INTERNATIONAL
Herald Tribune.

Published With The New York Times and The Washington Post

THE WORLD'S DAILY NEWSPAPER

ON THE RECORD

Mastering Reading and Language Skills with the Newspaper

Robert Hughes

National Textbook Company
a division of NTC/CONTEMPORARY PUBLISHING GROUP
Lincolnwood, Illinois USA

"Something Wrong with My Eyes" reprinted from the *Hartford Courant*.
"In Nagano, Cross-Cultural Tensions" reprinted by permission of Reuters.
Articles from the *International Herald Tribune* are reprinted by permission
of the International Herald Tribune, 181 avenue Charles-de-Gaulle,
92200 Neuilly-sur-Seine, France; The New York Times; and The Washington
Post, the copyright proprietors.

ISBN: 0-8442-0306-8

Published by National Textbook Company,
a division of NTC/Contemporary Publishing Group, Inc.,
4255 West Touhy Avenue,
Lincolnwood (Chicago), Illinois 60646-1975 U.S.A.
© 1999 NTC/Contemporary Publishing Group, Inc.

890 VL 0987654321

CONTENTS

INTRODUCTION

On the Record is a reading-skills text built around articles from the *International Herald Tribune*. Readers who are familiar with *Morning Edition* will be pleased to see this new volume featuring 16 recently published articles.

The *International Herald Tribune*, edited in Paris, France, is read around the world. Many of its articles originally appeared in *The New York Times* or *The Washington Post*. They are examples of the finest in American journalism. Other articles were written by *International Herald Tribune* journalists, who provide insightful coverage of happenings around the globe.

The articles in *On the Record* have been carefully selected for high interest, international cope, and varied subject areas. In this text, you will read about the secrets of a world-famous magician, the strange dining habits of the killer shark, a comedian who could tell more than eight jokes a minute, athletes who "compete" using simple exercise equipment, and people who cool off in the summer by eating incredibly hot food. News, business, science, sports, entertainment—these subjects and more are covered in the text. The articles provide fascinating facts on a wide range of topics, information you will enjoy reading and sharing.

As you explore the issues in *On the Record*, you will strengthen your reading skills. The exercises that accompany the articles are designed to help you better understand the articles' main points and their vocabulary and idioms. The reading strategies you learn can be applied to your independent reading of a wide range of texts, from magazines and popular fiction to textbooks and business reports.

Special attention is given to improving newspaper reading skills in the text's seven "Focus on the Newspaper" sections. The first Focus section provides an overview of the newspaper. The others, placed at the end of each section of the text, deal with specific parts of the newspaper or particular types of writing: "hard" news stories, features, opinion pieces, profiles, sports stories, reviews, business news, and more. The Focus sections describe the kinds of information you can expect to find in the newspaper and provide hands-on practice in recognizing and analyzing various types of articles.

The material accompanying each article is organized as follows:

Previewing the Article

- Introduces the topic of the article and provides background information helpful in understanding the article
- Provides discussion questions to stimulate interest in the article and to activate prior knowledge about the topic
- Suggests specific information to look for as you read

Getting the Message

- Focuses on key points of the article, using a variety of exercise types, including true/false and multiple-choice items
- Offers an opportunity to confirm your understanding of the article by comparing your answers with the Comprehension Check at the back of the book

Expanding Your Vocabulary

- Provides practice in determining the meanings of words and phrases through context
- Helps group related words (about occupations, sports, and other subjects) to aid in comprehension and retention of vocabulary
- Encourages analysis of both denotations and connotations of words

Working with Idioms and Expressions

- Defines key idioms and expressions from the article
- Provides practice in using idioms and expressions in context

Analysis of Key Features

Each lesson includes a section titled "Making Sense of Sentences," "Analyzing Paragraphs," or "Focusing on Style and Tone." These sections examine more-sophisticated elements of the article, such as the following:

- sentences that include comparisons, passive forms, appositives, and other elements of complex and compound sentences
- paragraph development and the ways in which various paragraphs relate to each other and to the main point of the article
- elements of style, such as the use of irony

Talking and Writing

- Suggests several topics relating to issues in the article for oral or written discussion
- Encourages thinking beyond the article to the implications and long-term significance of its message

We hope that you enjoy the articles in *On the Record* and the accompanying exercises and activities. We also hope that this text will inspire you to spend some time each day "seeing" the world through the newspaper.

How to Read the Newspaper for Information and Enjoyment

Daily newspapers offer you a whole world to explore. Within their pages, you will find articles that inform, educate, excite, anger, or concern you. By reading the newspaper, you can find out about what's happening throughout the world: locally, nationally, and internationally. In this Focus section, you will learn about some general features of newspapers to aid you in reading them on your own. You will also analyze your current newspaper reading habits.

Overview of the Newspaper

Newspapers use a number of devices to help their readers find information quickly:
- boxes listing articles, found on the front page of the paper or of a section
- an index (often on the front page or the second page)
- page headings
- headlines

Most newspapers are divided into sections, including news, business, and sports. The sections come in a regular order; for example, the sports section is often last. Sometimes newspapers have special sections, such as an entertainment section on the weekend.

You will notice that articles often begin with a *dateline*, or name of the place where the article was written. You'll find datelines from all over the world.

Exercise 1: The Organization of the Newspaper

A. Look at a recent issue of a newspaper. Circle some examples of the devices that help you find information.

B. Look over the newspaper you usually read. List the order of the sections.

Exercise 2: Locating Things in the Newspaper

Look through a newspaper for the following information. Then tell the location (the section number and page) where you found each item.

1. the weather forecast

2. the score of a sports event

3. a story about business conditions

4. a dateline from a European country

5. a headline that includes the name of a country

6. information about a cultural event

7. a letter to the editor

Your Newspaper Reading Habits

You will find many different types of articles in a newspaper. News articles are typically at the front of the paper: these report current news and political events. Articles expressing opinions and taking positions on current issues are on the opinion pages. Feature articles give background information about the news and may express the viewpoint of the writer. They may be found throughout the paper.

When you read a newspaper, do you often read just particular kinds of articles, such as sports pieces? Or do you usually look through the entire newspaper to find what interests you? In this section you will explore your reading habits so that you can make the best use of the newspaper.

Exercise 3: What Catches Your Interest?

Skim an entire newspaper, looking for articles that interest you. Read whatever catches your interest. On a separate sheet of paper, complete a chart like the following. Fill in the first two columns with information about each article you look at. Then check the appropriate column to show how much of the article you read.

Name of Article or Item	Type of Article or Item*	I Read the Headline Only	I Read the First Paragraph	I Quickly Skimmed It	I Read It Carefully

*Use these abbreviations: N = News story; F = Feature story; ED = Editorial/Opinion; C = Cartoon; P = Photo; A = Advertisement; O = other.

As you did the activity, did you read anything interesting that you might not have noticed if you had followed your regular reading habits? Repeat exercise 3 several times as you work through this book. Do you find your reading habits changing?

Exercise 4: Reviewing Your Newspaper Reading Habits

Think about the following questions. Write your thoughts in a notebook, or discuss them with a partner.

1. Do you follow the same pattern each time you read a newspaper? For example, do you always look at the back page first?

2. What kinds of articles do you usually read: "hard" news stories? sports stories? editorials? comics? Why?

3. How familiar are you with various sections of the newspaper? Can you find what you're looking for quickly?

4. What motivates you to read an article: your interest in the subject? a catchy headline? the length?

5. What is your main purpose in reading the newspaper? Does your purpose ever change?

6. Do you usually read the entire newspaper from front page to back page? If not, what are some reasons: lack of time? lack of interest? lack of familiarity with some topics? unfamiliar vocabulary?

7. Do you read more than one newspaper regularly? If so, what are the differences between the papers?

8. Do you think your newspaper reading habits will be the same in six months? in a year? Would you like to change your reading habits? Why or why not?

Analyzing Headlines

Headlines are designed to catch your eye and interest as you look through a newspaper. They typically summarize the focus of an article in a few words. Headlines help you predict the subject of an article and its main idea or viewpoint, so they are important in helping you use the newspaper for your own purposes.

Headlines pose special problems in reading. Often, short function words such as *be* and *the* are left out. Also, headlines often contain idioms, wordplay, or puns, because headline writers are trying to be clever and attract reader interest. Note the following types of headlines:

- *Straightforward headlines.* Many headlines make a clear, direct statement about the subject of the article. For example, in the Science/Health section of this text, "Evaluating Acupuncture: Medical Profession Is Divided" not only summarizes the information presented in the article but also suggests its balanced, objective tone. In the Sports section the headline "In Nagano, Cross-Cultural Tensions" explains the content of the story in a short phrase.

- *Headlines using wordplay*. One of the headlines in the Arts/Entertainment section is "Gender Gap at the Movies: Women in the Front Row." This headline begins with a straightforward announcement of the topic of the article. But the phrase after the colon uses wordplay. The phrase *in the front row* can mean "first" or "most prominent." But it also has a literal meaning that refers to the first row in a movie theater. It is a playful way to suggest that women's taste in films is becoming more of a factor in determining which films succeed. In the same section the headline "Poof! Questions About Magic Go Up in Smoke" is a clever way to compare the reporter's questions about magic to something that vanishes in a cloud of smoke in a magic act. Thus, the headline refers both to a magic trick and the content of the story.

- *Headlines requiring background knowledge*. In the Business section the headline *"L'Air de Jordan: Be like Mike, Smell like Mike"* assumes several things. The reader is supposed to recognize that the article has something to do with the famous basketball player Michael Jordan. The reader is also supposed to be familiar with a television commercial that uses the expression "Be like Mike." The first part of the headline assumes that the reader is familiar with the term *"L'air de . . . "* for perfumes and colognes. Another headline, "Mind Your Etiquette: The New Emily Post," in the Profiles section, assumes that the reader knows about the famous book on manners written by Emily Post. This headline is meaningless to readers who have never heard of the book. In *On the Record* the "Previewing the Article" sections provide a bridge for readers who might otherwise miss some references. The exercises following the article also help readers to notice and understand cultural allusions and idiomatic expressions.

Exercise 5: Behind the Headlines

Look through a newspaper and select four headlines. Predict the subject of each article from the information in the headline. Then read the article to find its subject. How many of your predictions were accurate? Show the results of this experiment by completing a chart like this one.

Headline	Predicted Subject	Actual Subject

Exercise 6: Make the Headlines

Cut three articles from a newspaper. Cut off and save the headlines. Trade your "beheaded" articles with a classmate's. Read the articles you receive, and write your own headlines for them. Then compare the headlines you and your partner wrote with the original ones the newspaper printed. In each pair, which headline is better? Why?

NEWS/FEATURES

1. Russians Are Laughing Again— at Themselves

Previewing the Article

"Laugh and the world laughs with you." This is an old way to express the truth that laughter unites people. However, the saying leaves out the fact that laughter also *separates* people: it separates the laughers from the ones being laughed at.

This feature article is about how the unifying and dividing power of laughter is demonstrated in the Russia of today. The old Soviet Union attempted to establish a "class-free" society. Thus, under the communist system, in their lives, ordinary people did not see the showy class distinctions common in capitalist societies. For example, Americans in big cities are accustomed to seeing the signs of spectacular wealth all around them: expensive cars, flashy clothes, and enormous houses. They even have a term for the buying of things for the purpose of showing social status: "conspicuous consumption."

But all this is new for Russians, who view the coming of sudden wealth to a few with some resentment. The newly rich fancy dressers and flashy spenders seem to be asserting themselves as "better" than others. In contrast, only a few years before, everyone was "equal." So Russian humor has shifted from the communist custom of mocking the government to the democratic custom of mocking the rich. And a new economic division, between the very rich and the common people, has appeared.

In democratic countries there is a long history of the common person laughing at the rich. The "have nots" like to make fun of the "haves." In the United States, for example, a century ago Mark Twain mocked European aristocracy in books such as *The Prince and the Pauper.* The tradition of this kind of humor continues today on American late-night television, where Jay Leno and David Letterman make fun of rich celebrities and politicians.

Before You Read

Discuss these questions.

1. Do you like jokes? Why or why not? Do you enjoy having friends tell you jokes? What is the last joke you heard?

2. Do you feel comfortable listening to a joke that makes fun of a group of people? Why or why not? Give some examples.

3. What is a "punch line"?

As You Read

As you read, look for the connection between Russia's "new rich" and politics.

Russians Are Laughing Again— at Themselves

Jokes Questioning Intelligence and Taste Ridicule New Rich

By Daniel Williams
Washington Post Service

1 MOSCOW—Then there was the one about the newly rich Russian who had smashed his car in a terrible accident.

2 "Oh, my Mercedes! Oh, oh, my poor Mercedes!" he cries.

3 A passer-by notices that the man's arm is missing. "Your car? So what!" he says. "Take a look at your arm!" The rich Russian gazes at where his arm used to be, then moans, "Ohhhh, my Rolex!"

4 As Russia has changed rapidly in the past six years, so has its sense of humor. Once, the political joke held sway, the secret jest that jabbed at 70 years of repressive regimes.

5 Stalin, Nikita Khrushchev, Leonid Brezhnev—especially the doddering Brezhnev of his later years—and Mikhail Gorbachev were the butts of stories told over the kitchen table to close friends out of earshot of the secret police.

6 But the communist era ended, and so did the fear. Somehow, it seemed, making fun of politicians didn't have the same kick.

7 Or at least not the kick being supplied by the newest wave of humor here: jokes told at the expense of New Russians.

8 New Russians is the name given to the fabulously wealthy, incredibly showy and— the jokes imply—very dumb beneficiaries of Russia's wild brand of capitalism.

9 Newspapers print them, and published collections are sold at railroad station newsstands for easy reading on weekend trips. (One publisher uses the logo of a Golden Toilet to distinguish his New Russian joke books from others.) Housekeepers buy cassettes of recorded jokes to listen to while gardening or cooking.

10 "There's a desire to laugh at the rich and a desire to laugh at the easy money being made in Russia, even though only a few are making it," said Yevgeni Petrossian, a leading comedian. "It's a classic defense of the underdog."

11 Mr. Petrossian is the author of a collection of Russian jokes told through the years. He updated the sixth edition to include the New Russian series.

12 "I think the first one I heard—everyone has heard it—was about two New Russians meeting on the street," he said. "One says, 'Look at this tie I bought in New York. $1,500!'"

13 "'What a fool!' answers the other. 'Here, you can get it for $2,000.'"

14 The transition from communist-era jokes to the era of democracy was anything but swift, Mr. Petrossian recalled. In 1992 and 1993, there were virtually no jokes. "Things were changing too fast, and times were too hard. No one knew what was funny or not," he said.

15 With the flowering of sudden wealth among the few, the New Russians emerged and provided an easy target. Their clothes are distinctive: for men, Italian suits with shoulder pads that a linebacker would envy; for women, miniskirts and long, high-heeled leather boots.

16 Mercedes-Benz and BMW are the preferred brands of car, although the other day, a Pontiac Trans Am convertible was spotted on Pushkin Square—in a city where winter often lasts nine months. Bodyguards are de rigueur, and they wear the same Italian suits.

17 Restaurants for New Russians are opulent and extremely expensive. The other day—and this is no joke—a waiter at an Italian restaurant in Moscow tried to explain to a customer why a run-of-the-mill Tuscan wine on the menu was so expensive.

18 "If we list it cheap," he said, "New Russians won't buy it."

19 Some observers consider the jokes not merely social but politically pointed because of the well-publicized close ties between the government and tycoons in Russia.

20 "There is an implied criticism," said Robert Coalson, who writes a column on language for the Moscow Times. "You could easily put into the jokes the name of some of the major millionaires with links to the Yeltsin government and get the same laughs."

21 Mr. Coalson, who also works as a consultant for regional newspapers in Russia, collected some jokes for a recent column, and the auto-accident tale was his favorite.

22 "That kind of black humor has a long tradition in Russia," he said. "Some of the jokes are pretty grim."

23 Most of the jokes about New Russians are unflattering. In a country in which

Sergei Karpukhin/The Washington Post

At the Moscow Country Club outside the capital, a Russian gives his wife some tips.

there is much contemplation of the mysterious Russian soul, these jokes suggest the New Russians have none. An example:

24 One day, the devil meets a New Russian and offers him anything he wants.

25 "I want a license to import anything I want free," the New Russian says. "I want oil fields. I want tax breaks. Now, what do I owe you?"

26 "Your soul," the devil responds lustily.

27 The New Russian scratches his head and thinks hard: "Uh . . . so what's the catch?" Poorer Russians—sometimes referred to as Old Russians in the jokes— apparently tend to regard the New Russians as likely criminals.

28 The inference is understandable, given the stream of stories about organized-crime killings and government-business corruption.

29 "Have you got a book on how to become rich?" a customer asks a clerk.

30 "Yes, it's called the Criminal Code," the clerk answers.

After reading the article, circle the best answer for each item.

1. This article is mainly about
   a. how political change in Russia has had negative social effects.
   b. how political change has brought about a new kind of joke in Russia.
   c. why Russians had no sense of humor during the Soviet years.

2. In the first joke about the accident victim (paragraphs 1–3), the line "Ohhhh, my Rolex!" is funny because
   a. the man was more worried about his watch than his own arm.
   b. the man wanted to buy a new watch right after a car accident.
   c. the passerby wanted the man's watch.

3. Before jokes about the rich, most Russian jokes were about
   a. movie stars.
   b. Americans.
   c. politicians.

4. One sign of how popular the jokes about the rich are is that
   a. joke books and recorded jokes on cassette are common.
   b. even the rich tell the jokes about themselves.
   c. no one tells any other kind of joke anymore.

5. The joke about the expensive tie (paragraphs 12–13) intends to show that New Russians
   a. do not know where to shop for cheaper clothes.
   b. are foolishly proud of spending money.
   c. do not like New York City.

6. The story about the waiter at an Italian restaurant in Moscow (paragraphs 17–18) is different from the other stories because it
   a. is not about the rich.
   b. took place during the Soviet years.
   c. is true.

7. The joke about the New Russian and the devil (paragraphs 24–27) shows that the new rich
   a. have no spiritual values.
   b. are clever.
   c. have little education.

Check your answers with the key on page 117. If you have made mistakes, reread the article to gain a better understanding of it.

II. Expanding Your Vocabulary

A. Getting Meaning from Context

Find each word in the paragraph indicated in parentheses. Use context clues to determine the meaning of the word. Choose the definition that fits the context.

1. smashed (1)	a. crashed, destroyed	b. driven far
2. moans (3)	a. says in surprise	b. cries in pain
3. doddering (5)	a. exciting	b. old and weak
4. wave (7)	a. a greeting	b. a trend
5. distinguish (9)	a. make different from	b. recognize
6. flowering (15)	a. gardening	b. growth
7. opulent (17)	a. fancy and luxurious	b. large
8. tycoon (19)	a. someone successful in business	b. a politician with an important job
9. unflattering (23)	a. not favorable	b. not humorous
10. inference (28)	a. something inferior	b. something concluded from known information

B. Defining Adverbs from the Article

The two most common uses of adverbs are to modify adjectives and verbs. The phrases from the article in column A have adverbs in italic type. Match each phrase in column A with the word or words in column B that have the same meaning. For context clues reread the indicated paragraphs of the article.

A

1. Russia "has changed *rapidly*" (4) means it has changed _____.

2. An "*incredibly* showy" (8) person is _____ showy.

3. "*Virtually* no jokes" (14) means _____ no jokes.

4. If the devil "responds *lustily*" (26), he responds _____.

5. If jokes "*apparently* tend" (27), they _____ tend.

B

a. unbelievably, very

b. energetically

c. fast

d. seemingly

e. nearly, almost

III. Working with Idioms and Expressions

Study the meanings of these idioms and expressions. A form of each one appears in the indicated paragraph of the article.

so what (3) Why should that be important?

hold sway (4) have power; be the main influence

out of earshot (5) too far away to be heard

easy money (10) money that is earned quickly and easily, often in large amounts

the underdog (10) weaker person who is often treated badly

run-of-the-mill (17) average, not special

tax break (25) an exception that allows a taxpayer to pay lower taxes

Terms Related to Jokes

jest (4) joke

jab (4) make a quick, painful blow, like a joke that hits out at, or criticizes, something or someone

butt of a story (5) object of a critical joke

make fun of (6) make unkind jokes about

black humor (22) humor that treats tragedy as absurd or does not take it seriously

Complete these sentences, using the idioms, expressions, and terms.

1. Ordinary Russians today like to _____ the rich New Russians.

2. Some corrupt businessmen in Russia make _____ through illegal arrangements with politicians.

3. The joke about the accident victim is an example of _____ , because it makes light of a tragic situation.

4. In comparison to rich, lucky New Russians, many Old Russians think of themselves as _____ .

IV. Making Sense of Sentences

Writers often want to put additional information in a sentence. They can do this by putting the information in parentheses or putting dashes around the information.

The additional information between the parentheses or dashes often does the following:

- gives a definition of something in the sentence or explains something in the sentence
- gives an added detail about something in the sentence
- gives the writer's attitude or opinion about information in the sentence

Example of dashes: Mercedes-Benzes and BMWs—both expensive German-made cars—are the preferred cars of Russia's new rich.

Example of parentheses: In the recent past, Russians aimed their jokes at their repressive regimes. (Communist governments had been in power since 1922.)

Look through the story for examples of dashes and parentheses. Write the number of the paragraph in which you find each of these examples.

1. _____ explains why it is surprising to find a convertible car in Moscow.

2. _____ gives an explanation of the term *Old Russians.*

3. _____ gives additional information about the joke books available in Russia.

4. _____ gives added information about a political leader.

5. _____ explains why a term with a negative meaning is used in the article.

V. Talking and Writing

Discuss the following topics. Then choose one of them to write about.

1. Do you ever tell jokes that are "at the expense of" a particular group of people? Of the following groups, which are considered acceptable to joke about and which are not: disabled people, lawyers, old people, ethnic groups, politicians, teachers?

2. What advice would you give someone about how to tell a joke well? What should be done in preparation? What are problems to avoid? How can a joke be made funnier with one's voice and gestures?

3. Who is your favorite comedian? What do you like about the subject matter of the comedian's jokes and the way the comedian tells the jokes?

4. Are jokes and humor different in different countries and cultures? What experiences have you had with such differences?

2. Into the Hot Pot: A Searing Experience

Previewing the Article

What is considered "news"? A classic answer is given in this silly newspaper headline: "Man Bites Dog." Since a story about such an event would be strange and unexpected, it would be newsworthy. A story about a dog biting a man, however, would hold no surprise for readers.

This feature article is in the "Man Bites Dog" category. It tells about the popularity in China of eating the hottest possible soup to get relief from horribly hot weather. The soup is "hot" both because of the spices in it and because of its temperature. On hot days most readers the world over do exactly the opposite of what these residents of Chongqing, China, do. In the United States, for example, most people regard air-conditioning and cold drinks on hot summer days as necessities of life. This Chinese idea of how to get relief from the heat would come as a surprise to most readers in the West.

Chinese people keep this old tradition of eating the hottest food on the hottest days, although their nation is experiencing many social and economic changes. Chongqing, like many cities all over China, is becoming more modern in a Western sense, with a more capital-istic economy and rapid economic growth. The city itself (known as Chungking when it was the capital of the Republic of China from 1937 to 1946) is the seventh largest in China, with a population of more than 2,800,000 people. It is a gray-walled city with a history that goes back more than 4,000 years. This fact may help explain why old traditions like eating hot soup survive in the modern, technological age.

Before You Read

Discuss these questions.

1. Read the headline. It is meant to remind the reader of the phrase "Out of the frying pan and into the fire." What does this expression mean? How would it apply to the diners in this article?

2. What do you do to get relief from the heat on a hot day? Does eating hot food to feel cool make sense to you?

3. What sorts of foods have you tried that are hot and spicy? Do you like such foods?

As You Read

Look for information about the history of the hot pot and how it is changing.

Into the Hot Pot: A Searing Experience

By Seth Faison
New York Times Service

1 CHONGQING, China—For a professional pool player, Meng Lang was pretty clumsy with chopsticks. He kept losing his grip on the chunks of pig's brain, which fell back into the iron pot of boiling oil and hot chili peppers.

2 Not that it mattered. The whole point of "hot pot," a tongue-searing experience that is a summer favorite in this city, is to bathe the morsels in a special hot, hot, hot concoction for as long as a diner can bear.

3 It may sound odd, but it's true: The hotter it gets outside, the more people in this corner of China like to eat the hottest food imaginable. There is no better way, many swear, to fight the sweltering heat.

4 "If you want to stay cool," Meng murmured between bites, once he finally got a handle on the food, "you have to get hot."

5 As China hurtles down the path of fast economic growth, so evident in the mishmash of construction underway in a smoggy and overcrowded city like Chongqing, some residents seem glad to cling to a few traditions. One of the most beloved, many residents say, is eating hot pot at the height of summer.

6 One recent evening, Meng met some friends for dinner shortly after sundown, as the temperature drifted not far from the day's peak of 39 degrees centigrade (102 degrees Fahrenheit) and an unbearable humidity hung in the air like a giant hot towel. For most mortals, simply walking down the street was enough to drench them in sweat.

7 Inside the Jin Jianglan Hot Pot Center, it was even hotter. There was no air-conditioning, on purpose, and the hearth at each table was like a small furnace. The experience was somewhat like being in a sauna, only one where people are eating.

8 Meng and his pals took off their shirts and hung them on a hook on the wall, as though it were time to get down to business, which in this case simply meant eating and sweating. So accustomed are they to the ritual, however, that none of the friends showed more than a thin bead of forehead perspiration until well into the meal.

9 "There is no way you can feel hot when you leave here, because every place else feels cool," said Li Xiaogang, who described himself half-jokingly as Meng's apprentice at the pool table, but who is also his business manager. "Here, try some cow's throat."

10 The choice of edibles at any traditional hot pot can seem daunting—calf's liver, pig's brain, and cow's throat are Li's favorites, though he'll sample a few vegetables, too. But the uninitiated may have difficulty distinguishing much, in terms of taste, beyond hot chili.

11 "The main thing is to put enough chili peppers in with the oil, so that it's hot," said Tang Minfang, the restaurant's manager, in a mild understatement. "Any traditional place will also add a splash of pig's blood, to give it body."

12 The recent appearance of fancy, air-conditioned eateries with red chintz drapes and pink tablecloths advertising themselves as hot pot restaurants seemed to offend Tang as deeply as if he were a proud guardian of a cultural relic.

13 "That's not real hot pot," he said, quite sternly. "They're trying to use the name of Chongqing hot pot, but it's all fake. They know nothing of real hot pot."

Nicolae Asciu/IHT

14 According to local lore, Chongqing hot pot evolved early this century among coolies whose back-breaking labor involved tugging riverboats upstream against the strong current of the Yangtze River, working in teams on the riverbanks. Underpaid and overworked, coolies could afford little for meals and often gathered around a fire and a common pot, into which they dipped any food they could get their hands on.

15 People in Chongqing, transliterated as Chungking when it was the wartime capital of China's Nationalist government, have been eating hot pot ever since, Tang said.

16 Back at the pool players' table, the conversation turned to important issues, like a future tournament.

17 "Is Fat Wang coming?" asked Meng, as he fished around in the pot for yet another misplaced animal part. "We have to make sure we don't go up against him."

18 Meng's wife came in and plopped down on a seat beside her husband.

19 "You haven't started sweating. Just begin?" she asked, as though this was a standard way to judge progress in a meal.

20 Another friend explained quietly that Meng's wife is the daughter of the district head of police, a big cheese by any measure. By extension, so is she, and since she married him last year, so is Meng.

21 Yet as they took turns dipping their chopsticks into the cauldron of hot sauce, Meng and his wife looked like any other Chongqing residents, preparing to sweat up a storm.

22 "Everyone likes hot pot," she said. "It's best in the summer, when it's hot."

I. Getting the Message

After reading the article, indicate whether each statement is true (**T**) or false (**F**). For help reread the paragraph(s) indicated in parentheses.

1. _____ This article begins with a description of the history of hot pot. (1)

2. _____ Eating hot pot on a hot day is a tradition that goes back hundreds of years. (14, 15)

3. _____ The dinner referred to in the article takes place in an average Chongqing family home. (7)

4. _____ People believe that eating hot pot will make them feel so warm that the hot weather will seem cool by comparison. (9)

5. _____ The people interviewed in the article found their food so hot that they needed to turn up the strong air-conditioning just to be comfortable. (8)

6. _____ People eating hot pot for the first time might think it tastes like hot chili. (10)

7. _____ In traditional hot pot, meat and chili peppers are the only ingredients. (10, 11)

8. _____ According to the manager of the hot-pot restaurant in the article, fancy new hot-pot restaurants are a good thing because they are helping to keep the tradition alive. (12, 13)

Check your answers with the key on page 117. If you have made mistakes, reread the article to gain a better understanding of it.

II. Expanding Your Vocabulary

A. Getting Meaning from Context

Find each word in the paragraph indicated in parentheses. Use context clues to determine the meaning of the word. Choose the definition that fits the context.

1. searing (headline)   a. memorable   b. very hot

2. clumsy (1)   a. awkward   b. experienced

3. sweltering (3)   a. very hot   b. a little warm

4. drifted (6)   a. moved slowly   b. moved very fast

5. daunting (10)   a. desirable   b. discouraging

6. eateries (12)   a. different foods   b. restaurants

7. sternly (13)   a. firmly, harshly   b. generously

8. tugging (14)   a. constructing   b. pulling

B. Finding Verbs with Similar Meanings

Find a verb with a similar meaning in the paragraph indicated in parentheses.

1. *insist to be true* (3) _____

2. *said quietly* (4) _____

3. *moves quickly* (5) _____

4. *make completely wet* (6) _____

5. *changed or developed slowly* (14) _____

6. be *able to pay for* (14) _____

III. Working with Idioms and Expressions

Study the meanings of these idioms and expressions. A form of each one appears in the indicated paragraph of the article.

lose one's grip on (1) no longer have control of something

get a handle on (4) gain control of something

at the height of (5) at the top or strongest point of something

get down to business (8) start doing something seriously

give something body (11) make something thicker and fuller

get one's hands on (14) obtain

go up against (17) oppose or play against in a competition

take turns (21) do in order, with one following the other in a regular pattern

(do) up a storm (21) (do) vigorously and enthusiastically

Answer these questions.

1. Why would it be difficult for you to *get your hands on* food needed to prepare the hot pot?

2. What would you expect the weather to be like if winter were *at its height*?

3. Near the end of the article, Meng Lang seems concerned about *going up against* Fat Wang. Is Fat Wang probably a strong or weak pool player?

4. Would an average American be likely to eat *up a storm* at a hot pot dinner?

5. Why would an average American be likely to *lose his or her grip on* chopsticks?

Paragraphs in newspaper stories are usually shorter than paragraphs in magazines, nonfiction books, and textbooks. Narrow newspaper columns make paragraphs that are standard in other places look long and uninviting to read. So, to help newspaper readers to get information quickly and to skim rapidly through the article, paragraphs in newspaper articles are typically short. Often this means that an important point is discussed through a number of paragraphs in the articles.

Look back at the article and circle the best answer for each item.

1. Paragraphs 1–5 do all the following except
    a. explain what hot pot is.
    b. give a history of hot pot.
    c. introduce the reader to a hot-pot eater.

2. Paragraphs 6–9 introduce the reader to the dinner at the restaurant by doing all the following except
    a. introducing the reader to the restaurant setting.
    b. explaining the conditions hot-pot lovers enjoy.
    c. discussing the cost of a dinner in a hot pot.

3. Paragraphs 10–11 discuss the ingredients of hot pot in order to do all the following except
    a. show how surprisingly odd the ingredients are.
    b. give the reader good directions on how to make hot pot at home.
    c. explain how hot pot tastes.

4. Paragraphs 12–15 explain the history of hot pot by doing all the following except
    a. noting that poor workers created hot pot early in the 20th century.
    b. contrasting new hot-pot restaurants with traditional ones.
    c. showing how important hot-pot restaurants are in the Chinese restaurant industry.

5. Paragraphs 16–19 explain all the following except
    a. what the hot-pot diners discussed at the table.
    b. the standard way that diners judge progress in a meal.
    c. how successful Meng Lang was as a pool player.

6. Paragraphs 20–22 do all the following except
    a. explain the social status of Meng and his wife.
    b. show that hot pot is popular among all social classes.
    c. explain what other dishes are popular in Chongqing.

V. Talking and Writing

Discuss the following topics. Then choose one of them to write about.

1. Hot pot is a traditional Chinese meal. What traditional meals do you enjoy? Are they part of an ethnic, national, or religious tradition?

2. Do you like the cuisine (the style of cooking) of any country other than your own? Do you like going to restaurants (often called "ethnic" restaurants) that serve such food?

3. One of the biggest single sections in any bookstore is the cookbook section. Why is this so? How many cookbooks are there in your home? How often do you use them?

Focus on the Newspaper

Most people read a daily newspaper to find out what is happening in their community, their city, and their country, as well as around the globe. Newspapers have daily headlines and accompanying articles about the most important events affecting readers' lives. Whether it's a development in international or national politics, the success of a space mission, or the result of an important election, the news pages present the important facts on the subject.

Hard News Articles

Typically the "hard" news stories are on the front pages of newspapers. *Hard,* or *pure,* news stories report basic facts about an event or situation. Here are some essential characteristics that distinguish pure news articles:

- They report the facts, usually without giving the writer's viewpoint.
- They are usually short and to the point.
- They are organized to present all the important information in the first few paragraphs.

Most hard news articles follow a standard format. The lead (opening) paragraphs provide the most important information. The reader can read the first few paragraphs and find the answers to the five key "W" questions:

- *who*
- *what*
- *where*
- *when*
- and sometimes *why* or *how*

Thus, by skimming the lead, the reader can quickly get the main idea of a story and decide whether to read on.

Objective details about the story follow the lead, in descending order of importance. The article ends with the least important information. Often, this is historical background about the people, places, or events involved in the story. These concluding paragraphs can be cut if the newspaper needs the space for another article.

Exercise 1: The News in Depth

Choose a major news article from a daily newspaper. Read the article carefully. Then analyze it by answering the questions in the box titled "Analyzing a News Article."

Analyzing a News Article

1. Who wrote the article? In what city, state, and country did the story originate?

2. Does the article answer the five "W" questions in the first few paragraphs? What are the answers?

3. Does the article include all the information you want to know about the topic? If not, what is missing?

4. Does a photo or an illustration accompany the article? If so, what information does it provide? Is it clear? Is it interesting? Does it help the reader understand the main point of the article?

5. Can you detect any slant or viewpoint in the article—for example, in word choice or selection of facts?

6. Does the information in this article differ in any way from what you have heard on the radio, seen on television, or read in another newspaper about the same event? If so, what do you think is the reason for the difference?

7. Does the article deal with a controversial issue? If so, are the opposing points of view given equal space and objective presentation? Can you tell which side the journalist favors?

8. Do you consider this article a good example of clear, objective news reporting? If not, why not?

9. What are the strengths and weaknesses of the article?

10. If an editor had asked you to write this news story, what would you have done differently?

Feature Stories

Feature stories are quite different from hard news stories in both purpose and style. News stories present, as objectively as possible, the facts about the latest news events. Feature stories have a wide range of goals. Some feature stories explain, interpret, or provide background. Others (such as the two feature stories in this section, "Russians Are Laughing Again—at Themselves" and "Into the Hot Pot: A Searing Experience") tell of interesting, unusual events or trends that may be interesting or entertaining to the reader. Feature stories sometimes have emotional, personal, or humorous slants. Some are written in a distinctive style.

While some feature stories are related to major news events of the day (for example, a story analyzing the unhappy childhood of a person accused of murder), other topics reappear predictably. On any holiday or historical anniversary, newspaper readers expect to find feature stories related to that subject. In the United States, Father's Day inspires articles about famous (or infamous) fathers. In newspapers around the world, the fiftieth anniversaries of important World War II battles and bombings led to features about people who experienced these events.

Exercise 2: Categorizing Stories as Hard News or Features

With a classmate look through the first six pages of a daily newspaper. Skim the first few paragraphs of each article and decide whether it is a hard news story or a feature. Discuss what elements of the article helped you to classify it.

Exercise 3: The Feature Story in Depth

Select a feature story from your local newspaper. After reading it carefully, answer the questions in the box titled "Analyzing a Feature Story."

Analyzing a Feature Story

1. What does the first paragraph accomplish? Is its main purpose to answer the five "W" questions or to attract the reader's attention?

2. Does the article end with less important, background information, or does it end with a "punch"?

3. Does this feature story relate to a news event covered elsewhere in the paper? If so, what is that event? If not, why has the story been printed?

4. Can you detect the author's attitude toward the story? If so, describe it.

5. Does the article explain something that you didn't understand before? If so, what does it explain?

6. Do you have an emotional reaction to the story? Do you find it funny or sad? Does it make you angry?

7. Does the article make you want to do something, such as change your behavior in some way or become involved in a cause?

OPINION

1. Something Wrong with My Eyes

Have you ever doubted the public statements of important people in the news? For example, have you ever heard a politician say that "unemployment is low" while you were having difficulty finding a job? Have you ever heard that "food prices are going down" when you were having trouble paying your bills? Then you have experienced what the author of this article discusses: the gap between the words of people with power and the realities of living for everybody else.

The 1990s have been a time of important, hopeful changes for the United States. The Soviet Union, the enemy of the West in the Cold War, has collapsed. The federal budget is balanced or nearly so. Unemployment is low. But all these positive facts, the author of this opinion essay says, have not turned into happy realities for everyone. In fact, he says, the ones who have benefited the most from all these changes are "them"—the politicians and business leaders—not "us," the vast majority of ordinary people.

This article is a good example of one of the classic functions of a newspaper: to criticize and question the government. A traditional term for journalists is "the Fourth Estate," meaning an informal body critical of the established political order. Newspapers have always acted as a check on government, as the eyes of the people watching the politicians at work.

Before You Read

Discuss these questions.

1. Do you read opinion essays, editorials, or columns of opinion in the newspaper? Why or why not? If you have a favorite columnist, what is it that you particularly like about his or her writing?

2. What do you know about these topics in the news: gasoline taxes, corporate "downsizing," defense spending, and cuts in welfare? Have you ever been surprised by news stories about these issues?

3. Are you familiar with the common phrase used in conversations, "*They* say that . . ." Who do people usually mean by "they"?

As You Read

As you read, underline any reference that the author makes to *eyes* or *seeing*. Why does the author repeat such terms? Does this repetition make the essay more effective and better writing? How?

Something Wrong with My Eyes

By Denis Horgan
The Hartford Courant

1 HARTFORD, Connecticut—Maybe it's my weary old peepers, but I never seem to see things.

2 They cut the gasoline tax and I don't see the price go down. Instead the price goes up. No matter what happens the price goes up, and no matter what happens the price never goes down.

3 Cold weather? It drives up the price. Hot weather? It drives up the price. Cut taxes? They raise the price to pay for the change. When there is an international crisis, they run up the price of oil in anxiety; when the crisis goes away, the price stays up. When we are in an oil glut, the price goes up instead of down.

4 Everywhere, big companies lay off half the work force, wrecking the lives of thousands of employees, and I don't see where anyone's better off for it except for a few bosses. Not the customers. Not the public. Surely not those laid off nor those left behind.

5 They say I should see that the stockholders are better off, but what I see is that they get a quarter or 50 cents more in dividends, a small increase in stock price. And for that people's lives are destroyed, service is gutted, products and reputations are diminished. So someone can make pennies and executives can make millions. Fortunately, there is at least a Hereafter where that will be redressed.

6 The Cold War is over and I don't see where the peace dividend is. We pumped trillions into defense when there was someone to defend against, but I don't see where there's a need to pump trillions more into gigantic submarines and monster bombers with no knowable use and into military alliances with no known purpose anymore. We could have hoped that some of the savings might show up in helping neglected corners of the society, but I don't see it.

7 They cut the taxes of the wealthy, telling us that's good for us all, and I don't see where that helps anyone but the wealthy. They say that we will all benefit when the rich get around to trickling it down to us later, but I never see that happening. We forever await the grace of the privileged without ever much getting it.

8 Meantime, we can see quite clearly that there is less for support efforts for those who need them.

9 Companies cut services while making bloated profits, and no one sees any of that coming back to the sap customer paying new fees and higher prices and getting poorer products and less support than ever before.

10 I don't see that those efficiencies very often benefit the people paying the bill. Employee rolls are skinnied up and replaced with part-timers and temps and others on the cheap—but when was the last time the savings showed up on the price tag? I don't see it happening very often.

11 We are told we will save money by not helping those who need help, and people actually will be better off for being poorer, but I don't see either happening. Do you have more money in your pocket because they've whittled the welfare funds? I don't. Maybe when we finally get it we'll spend it on cheaper gas.

12 Do you see all those jobs that don't exist being filled by people who were straight-arming away jobs in favor of keeping the peanuts they get from the dole? Neither do I. What I think I see is a mood where people of no wealth become people of no value and, thereafter, are invisible. Unseen.

13 To thundering self-praise, they tell us they've balanced the national budget which will make things better while, at the same time, spreading such tax advantages and college aid and various bits of boodle as to turn this into the Promised Land. Great. But maybe the promises are so seldom kept that you will pardon the squint as I keep on the lookout for the thing to happen.

14 From the left and from the right costly pledges of change fly only to produce more of the same, helping mostly and only those already with advantage and authority.

15 They tell us we will see it get better. Someday. Maybe I need new glasses.

After reading the article, circle the best answer for each item.

1. The writer thinks it is strange that even though the gasoline tax was cut, the price of gas
    a. has stayed the same.
    b. has gone up.
    c. is going down.

2. When workers are laid off or fired, the people who are supposed to benefit are
    a. the workers' families.
    b. the politicians.
    c. stockholders.

3. The author thinks that because the Cold War is over, spending on
    a. weapons should go down.
    b. atomic research should go up.
    c. welfare should go down.

4. The writer asserts that cuts in benefits to people on welfare has meant
    a. more money in the pockets of taxpayers.
    b. that many more people who used to be on welfare are now working.
    c. that neither taxpayers nor people on welfare seem to benefit.

5. When the writer concludes, "Maybe I need new glasses," he really means
    a. his eyes are weak.
    b. the truth is different from what "they" say it is.
    c. he doubts his own thinking.

Check your answers with the key on page 117. If you have made mistakes, reread the article to gain a better understanding of it.

II. Expanding Your Vocabulary

Getting Meaning from Context

Find each word in the paragraph indicated in parentheses. Use context clues to determine the meaning of the word. Choose the definition that fits the context.

1. weary (1)	a. tired	b. full of tears
2. glut (3)	a. an oversupply	b. overpricing
3. gutted (5)	a. extended over a wider area	b. destroyed the essential parts of

4. diminished (5)	a. made clearer	b. lowered
5. redressed (5)	a. clothed again	b. made fair
6. pumped (6)	a. poured into	b. took out
7. privileged (7)	a. the rich, lucky few	b. the unemployed
8. bloated (9)	a. very difficult	b. very big

III. Working with Idioms and Expressions

Study the meanings of these idioms and expressions. A form of each one appears in the indicated paragraph of the article.

drive up (3) push upward, increase

lay off (4) cut a job so the company can reduce costs

be better off (4) have more money and live more comfortably

trickle down (7) move slowly down, referring to an economic theory, popular during the administration of Ronald Reagan, that if rich individuals and corporations are taxed at a lower rate, they will reinvest money in ways that benefit everyone

skinny up (10) made thinner by reducing the numbers or amount

on the cheap (10) in the least expensive way possible

straight-arm away (12) push away forcefully

the left (14) those who are politically liberal

the right (14) those who are politically conservative

Complete these sentences, using the idioms and expressions. Use the correct forms of the verbs.

1. Since many companies today seek to reduce their workforce to save money, many

   workers are afraid that their companies might _____ them

   _____.

2. Some economists think that the profits of the rich can _____ to

   even the poor, but other economists question the idea.

3. No one seems to know what _____ the price of gasoline, but the

   price seems to rise no matter how the nation's economy is doing.

IV. Analyzing Paragraphs

One device the author of this essay uses is to repeat the word *they*. This word is often used in conversation to mean people in general or common opinion. Though the word in this essay is meant to refer to "people in power," it actually has specific meanings that change from paragraph to paragraph. In some paragraphs *they* refers to "politicians." In others it means "corporate executives." The context makes it possible for the reader to figure out which group the *they* refers to.

In this exercise reread the paragraph indicated and find the word *they*. Then put a check mark on the line underneath either "Politicians" or "Corporate Executives." If *they* refers to both, check both columns.

	Politicians	Corporate Executives
1. Paragraph 2	_____	_____
2. Paragraph 3	_____	_____
3. Paragraph 5	_____	_____
4. Paragraph 7	_____	_____
5. Paragraph 13	_____	_____
6. Paragraph 15	_____	_____

V. Talking and Writing

Discuss the following topics. Then choose one of them to write about.

1. The author of this article has opinions about a variety of issues. Which particular ones do you agree with? Which ones do you disagree with?

2. A major idea of this article is that political and economic change benefits mainly the rich or people who have power. Is this true? Can you think of any evidence to the contrary?

3. If the federal government ever manages to have a budget *surplus*, that is, money left over after all the necessary spending is done, what do you think should be done with this money? Why?

2. Smoking's Ravages: 'Look What It's Done to Me'

Previewing the Article

How powerful can an addiction to smoking be? As this opinion essay reveals, the habit can capture even the most brilliant and creative people. Although people know about smoking's role in causing cancer, heart disease, and emphysema, many do not want to—or cannot—quit. And among these people are some whose helplessness in the face of their addiction seems ironic in view of their tremendous success in life.

The writer's immediate source for the article is a *memoir*, a book containing autobiographical stories, by a surgeon. This surgeon has spent much of his professional career battling smoking as a cause of cancer. The book, among other things, tells of three famous men and the doctor's own unsuccessful attempts to get them to stop the habit. Here is some information on these men:

- *Yul Brynner* (1920–1985) was an actor best known for his portrayal of the king in *The King and I*, both on the stage originally (1951–1954) and in the film (1956). He also played lead roles in famous films such as *The Ten Commandments* (1956) and *The Magnificent Seven* (1960). His stamina and onstage presence—he won a special Tony Award at age 65 for a revival of *The King and I* —were in ironic contrast to his lack of power over his cigarette habit.

- *Alan Jay Lerner* (1918–1986) wrote the words, and Frederick Lowe wrote the music, to some of the greatest Broadway musicals—among them *My Fair Lady* (1956) and *Camelot* (1960). In addition, he worked with Leonard Bernstein on the musical *1600 Pennsylvania Avenue* (1976).

- *Leonard Bernstein* (1918–1990) was a conductor, composer, and pianist. His best-known work as a composer is the musical *West Side Story*, the film version of which won ten Academy Awards in 1961.

Before You Read

Discuss these questions.

1. Why do people begin to smoke? How difficult is it to stop?

2. Have you ever tried to convince someone to stop smoking? What happened?

3. As recently reported in the news, the government and tobacco companies have been involved in negotiations. The industries want limitations on lawsuits against them from smokers in return for agreeing to restrictions on cigarette advertising. Describe the cartoon accompanying the article. What is the figure on the ground in front of the gravestone doing?

As You Read

As you read the article, look for the quotation in the headline, "Look what it's done to me." Who said this and to whom?

Smoking's Ravages: 'Look What It's Done to Me'

By Bob Herbert
The New York Times

1 NEW YORK—Dr. William Cahan remembers dropping by the dressing room of Yul Brynner during the original run of "The King and I" in the early 1950s. "You could barely see that famous bald head through the cloud of cigarette smoke," said Dr. Cahan, a renowned cancer surgeon and at the time the son-in-law of Mr. Brynner's co-star, Gertrude Lawrence.

2 "When you saw him up on the stage with his bare chest, he looked indestructible. But he smoked four or five packs a day. I used to tell him the same thing I told everybody, 'For God's sake, cut it out.'"

3 Dr. Cahan would go on to become the senior attending surgeon at the Memorial Sloan-Kettering Cancer Center, where he dubbed his operating room "Marlboro country." He continued trying to persuade Mr. Brynner to give up cigarettes. In his memoir, "No Stranger to Tears," Dr. Cahan quoted the actor as saying: "Don't worry, Bill. They'll never get me."

4 During a tour of the hospital last week, and later over lunch, Dr. Cahan talked of the many celebrities he has known—many of them close personal friends—who have succumbed to cigarette-related diseases.

5 He told the story of a flight he took from Boston to New York in the 1980s with Leonard Bernstein and the lyricist Alan Jay Lerner.

6 Mr. Bernstein was chain-smoking, as usual. But an obviously jittery Mr. Lerner was trying to quit. He bit his nails, fingered a string of worry beads and talked about how guilty he felt at having so much trouble cutting cigarettes loose.

7 Mr. Lerner finally quit in 1986, but it was too late. A suspicious shadow on an X-ray taken just a few months later turned out to be lung cancer. It was inoperable. Pneumonia developed and Mr. Lerner was admitted to Sloan-Kettering's intensive care unit.

8 A young nurse on duty one night said, "I know this Mr. Lerner is very sick, but now I think he's hallucinating." When a senior nurse asked why, the young nurse replied, "He says he wrote 'My Fair Lady.'"

9 Dr. Cahan and Mr. Lerner had a big laugh over that the next day. But time was running out. "Alan called Lenny," Dr. Cahan said, "and tried to get him to quit.

He said: 'Lenny, please. Look what it's done to me.'"

10 Mr. Lerner died in June 1986, Mr. Bernstein in October 1990. In November 1990, Dr. Cahan wrote: "So they got Lenny, too, those patrons of the arts. To see him now reduced to dust by two lousy packs of cigarettes a day . . ."

11 The tobacco companies have succeeded so far in having it both ways.

12 When they are trying to entice you to smoke, they spend billions upon billions of dollars to make smoking seem like the most glamorous, adventurous, pleasurable and sexy pastime imaginable. When a smoker, riddled with disease and dying in great pain, goes into court for redress, the companies cry foul. It's your fault, they say. You must have known smoking was dangerous. Everybody knows it.

13 In fact, most smokers find themselves trapped by the following insidious combination: Smoking is extremely pleasurable for large numbers of people. Nicotine, despite the bizarre testimony of tobacco executives, is highly addictive. Cigarettes are relentlessly advertised—men, women and children are bombarded from birth to death with highly effective overt and subliminal messages that smoking is good. And, finally, most people, young and old, live their lives to some degree in a state of denial. Cancer? It won't happen to me.

14 When Dr. Cahan saw Yul Brynner for the last time, in the mid-1980s, the actor

was in a wheelchair, on his way to a radiation treatment at Memorial Sloan-Kettering. He had been diagnosed with lung cancer and the disease had spread to his spine. The two men chatted for a few minutes. As he was about to be wheeled away, Mr. Brynner turned and looked up at Dr. Cahan. In a hoarse voice, he said, "Why the hell didn't I listen to you?"

15 Mr. Brynner died on Oct. 10, 1985. A memorial service was held at the Shubert Theater. Among the eulogists was Alan Jay Lerner.

I. Getting the Message

After reading the article, indicate whether each statement is true (**T**) or false (**F**).

1. _____ Yul Brynner was a heavy smoker when he appeared in *The King and I* in the 1950s.

2. _____ The writer of the article interviewed Dr. Cahan in person.

3. _____ Alan Jay Lerner died four years before Leonard Bernstein.

4. _____ The writer believes that the tobacco companies show both the positive and negative effects of smoking in their cigarette advertising.

5. _____ The writer of the article thinks that most people who smoke realize that they will die of lung cancer sooner or later.

6. _____ One reason that the writer gives for people's smoking is that nicotine, an ingredient in tobacco, is something that people can't give up easily.

7. _____ The writer suggests, but does not say directly, that Yul Brynner died of lung cancer caused by smoking.

8. _____ The article suggests that smoking is an odd habit since no one enjoys it.

Check your answers with the key on page 117. If you have made mistakes, reread the article to gain a better understanding of it.

II. Expanding Your Vocabulary

A. Getting Meaning from Context

Find each word in the paragraph indicated in parentheses. Use context clues to determine the meaning of the word. Choose the definition that fits the context.

1. renowned (1)	a. rich	b. well-respected
2. indestructible (2)	a. strong	b. dangerous
3. dubbed (3)	a. hurt	b. named
4. jittery (6)	a. happy	b. nervous
5. hallucinating (8)	a. experiencing things that are not real	b. becoming more seriously ill
6. entice (12)	a. criticize	b. attract
7. insidious (13)	a. attractive but with a harmful effect	b. complicated but slowly getting easier
8. relentlessly (13)	a. without a stop	b. expensively

B. Identifying Categories of Words

Find the word or phrase that doesn't belong in each category.

1. people who work in a hospital

   doctor　　　　　**surgeon**　　　　**lyricist**　　　　**nurse**

2. words associated with live theater

   dressing room　**stage**　　　　**original run**　　**memorial service**

3. serious medical problems

   testimony　　　**disease**　　　**cancer**　　　　**pneumonia**

4. places where medical treatment is given

   operating room　**flight**　　　　**hospital**　　　**intensive care unit**

5. parts of the body

   lung　　　　　**spine**　　　　**beads**　　　　**nails**

III. Working with Idioms and Expressions

Study the meanings of these idioms and expressions. A form of each one appears in the indicated paragraph of the article.

drop by (1) visit briefly

cut something out (2) stop a habit

get someone (3, 10) defeat or kill someone

chain-smoking (6) continuous, uninterrupted smoking

cut something loose (6) get rid of something

on duty (8) at work and actively responsible

reduce to dust (10) kill

have it both ways (11) win or succeed no matter the outcome of a problem

cry foul (12) accuse of wrongful behavior

Answer the following questions.

1. Why do many smokers find it so difficult to *cut out* smoking?

2. Is it polite to *drop by* a hospital room if a friend is staying there?

3. If someone is *chain-smoking*, is the person smoking a little or a lot?

4. Do you think it is fair for tobacco companies to *cry foul* when dying smokers hold them responsible for their condition?

IV. Focusing on Style and Tone

In opinion articles, writers often use words that carry strong meanings, or connotations. The meanings can be either positive or negative. Writers sometimes use such words because the writers are taking a stand, and such language helps convey their attitudes.

The tobacco companies' position has been *questioned* by several antismoking groups. *(neutral)*

The tobacco companies' position has been *attacked* by several antismoking groups. *(strong verb)*

The tobacco companies' position has resulted in *an outcry* from several antismoking groups. *(strong noun)*

Answer these questions. Use a dictionary to find the meanings of the words.

1. In paragraph 12 what adjectives are used to describe the way smoking is presented in advertisements? What connotations do those adjectives have—positive ones or negative ones? Do you think that the adjectives are appropriate to describe the way smoking is portrayed in advertising?

2. In paragraph 13 the author says that the public is *relentlessly bombarded* with smoking advertisements. What does this suggest about the frequency of smoking advertising? What does it suggest about the author's attitude toward the advertising?

3. In paragraph 13 the adjective *insidious* is used to describe a combination of factors that lead people to smoke. What connotation does the word *insidious* have? How does the word suggest the author's attitude to smoking?

4. In paragraph 13 the author of the article uses the adjective *bizarre* to describe the testimony of tobacco company executives about the effects of nicotine. What can you conclude that tobacco company executives say about nicotine and addiction? How does the word suggest the attitude of the author of the article toward tobacco companies?

V. Talking and Writing

Discuss the following topics. Then choose one of them to write about.

1. Have you ever tried to break a bad habit, like smoking or drinking or eating too much of the wrong kinds of food? Describe your attempts to stop. How successful were you?

2. In the United States preventing children and teenagers from starting to smoke is a special problem. Why do so many young people smoke? What steps, if any, should the government take to prevent them?

Focus on the Newspaper

News stories are *objective* and do not overtly express a viewpoint. However, most newspapers have special pages reserved for presenting *subjective* material. These *opinion* pages contain several types of articles.

- **Editorials** express the opinions of the newspaper's editorial board and of other journalists who write for the paper. Often a newspaper is known for having a certain political slant, or viewpoint. For example, it may tend to favor a particular political party, or it may generally agree with a conservative or liberal outlook. This slant is usually expressed in the newspaper's editorials.

   Where can you find editorials? They are printed on a page called the editorial page, which is usually located toward the back of the paper's first section. Editorials are printed below the newspaper's *masthead* (which includes the name of the paper, its publisher, and its editors). Most editorials are printed without bylines (names of the writers).

- **Letters to the Editor** also appear on the editorial page in most papers. They are submitted by readers who want to state their views on public affairs. These letters often contain responses to news and opinion pieces that have previously appeared in the paper. Sometimes they tell "the other side of the story" or correct the paper's errors.

- **Columns** are written under a byline and express a certain writer's point of view. This point of view is not necessarily the opinion of the paper's editorial board. Big-city newspapers commonly carry the work of several columnists with somewhat different perspectives or areas of interest. Syndicated columnists have their columns published in many papers in many places. Guest columnists often include people who are not journalists but who have expertise in some field currently in the news. They present explanations and opinions about matters of current concern.

- **Political cartoons** use art to express a point of view on the issues in the news.

The newspaper does not limit all expressions of opinion to the opinion pages. The editorial pages deal mainly with the major news events and government actions. Opinions on other matters are scattered throughout the newspaper.

- **Reviews** provide evaluations of new books, plays, concerts, movies, and art exhibits. Many people read newspaper reviews before deciding how to spend their leisure time.

- **Columns** in the business, sports, and other sections provide analyses, opinions, and predictions. Thus, newspapers provide opinions on many facets of life—including politics, finance, culture, entertainment, and athletics.

Editorials and Columns

Whereas a headline in the news section might read "New Government Bill on Education," the opinion section would contain articles that evaluate the new education bill. A headline in the opinion section might read "Revisions Needed to Make Education Policy Effective." The headline and accompanying article present a judgment on the event. Taking a clear position on an issue is what distinguishes opinion articles from other articles in a newspaper.

Sometimes opinion pages present opposing views on the same news event: "Bad Planning on Education Policy," one article may read; another may say "Education Bill a Good First Step."

Exercise 1: What's the Opinion?

Analyze an editorial or column by answering the questions in the box titled "Analyzing an Editorial or Column."

Analyzing an Editorial or Column

1. Who wrote the article? Does it express the opinion of an individual or of the newspaper? How do you know?

2. What key words in the headline or first paragraph let you know the opinion expressed in the article?

3. What issue is discussed in the article?

4. What is the opinion of the newspaper or the columnist about the issue?

5. What reasons does the newspaper or columnist give to support the opinion?

6. What is your opinion on the issue?

Letters to the Editor

The Letters to the Editor section provides readers with a place to express their ideas on issues in the news or on the opinions expressed in the newspaper.

Exercise 2: What Are People Talking About?

Look at current issues of a newspaper for letters to the editor. List three subjects that currently interest people, judging from the letters to the editor.

Exercise 3: Get into the News

Write a short letter to the editor. Choose a subject in the news about which you have an opinion. Remember to express a clear main idea and provide reasons to support your opinion.

Exercise 4: Political Cartoons

Find a political cartoon in a current newspaper. Answer the questions in the box titled "Analyzing a Political Cartoon."

Analyzing a Political Cartoon

1. Who drew the cartoon?

2. Who or what is pictured in the cartoon?

3. Is there a caption on the cartoon? Do the characters say anything? How do the words help you understand the cartoon?

4. What issue is presented in the cartoon?

5. What position does the cartoonist take on the issue?

6. Is the cartoon humorous or satirical? Explain your answer.

7. Did you find the cartoon hard to understand? If so, what information about current events do you need to understand the cartoon?

Exercise 5: Do You Get It?

Clip a different political cartoon from a recent newspaper. Discuss your cartoons in small groups. Use the questions in "Analyzing a Political Cartoon" to help you discuss each cartoon's meaning.

1. 'Cubes' Vie with 'Caves' in Offices

People have strong feelings about where they live, and an office is where many people spend much of their day. That is why this article, about two opposing ways of designing office space, should be of interest to many readers.

The traditional office is a network of "caves"—that is, closed-in offices with doors. The offices are arranged according to a worker's status in the company: top executives have big caves in the corners with windows on two sides; lower workers have smaller caves leading up to the corners, some with windows and some without. This arrangement, however, is expensive, for much floor space is required, and it does not promote communication among workers.

Opposed to this system is the one that uses "cubes," or cubicles—minioffices that have low walls and no doors and are arranged more or less democratically. In this environment everybody has equal space and an equal lack of privacy. The arrangement saves money and encourages teamwork and, incidentally, permits the boss to keep an eye on what everybody is doing.

The debate over which arrangement is best arouses passion, for it involves opposing ways of living, even differences in personality type. Do you like to live in an open space, or do you like to have separate rooms for different activities? More important for business, it also involves opposing theories about how workers can be most productive: are workers creative individualists (cave dwellers), or are they teammates (cubists)?

Before You Read

Discuss these questions.

1. Do you work in a cubicle? Explain its advantages and disadvantages. If you don't, what do you *think* its advantages and disadvantages are?

2. Find the term *fault line* in the subtitle of this article. What does a "fault line" usually refer to? What kind of violent activity is associated with a fault line? Where is there a famous fault line in the United States?

3. What do you know about the two corporations Microsoft and Intel? How important are they in the world of high technology?

As You Read

As you read, look for the answer to this question: What kind of work area does the chairman of the Intel Corporation have?

'Cubes' Vie with 'Caves' in Offices

Debate's Fault Line: Microsoft vs. Intel

By Steve Lohr
New York Times Service

1 NEW YORK—Bill Rouady, 32, a software programmer, speaks of his craft in the accepted vernacular of modern business. Teamwork, cooperation and shared knowledge, he explains, are essential ingredients of success.

2 This open style of work, insists Mr. Rouady, an employee of Netscape Communications Corp., is best done in an open setting—where workers are separated only by low partitions instead of being walled off behind closed doors in individual offices.

3 "The programming code we write has to work together seamlessly, so we should work together seamlessly as well," he said.

4 In corporate America as a whole, these are mainstream views. But in the high-technology world, from Silicon Valley to Seattle, Mr. Rouady's comments are fighting words. It is a contentious issue, with beliefs fervently held on both sides. Pick your workplace: open plan or enclosed office.

5 Phrasing the debate another way, it's cube vs. cave.

6 It is the issue that splits the computer industry's most powerful partnership, the so-called Wintel duopoly, named for Microsoft Corp.'s Windows software and Intel Corp.'s microchips.

7 Intel is unflinchingly cubist, a stance the company adopted shortly after its founding in 1968. Its open-plan layout was embraced in the name of teamwork and egalitarian values, as an explicit rejection of the old-line hierarchy associated with traditional corporations.

8 Intel has no executive dining rooms, no reserved parking places and no exceptions to the cubes-for-all policy. Because of growth, the crowding at the company's Santa Clara, California, headquarters has increased, so cube sizes have shrunk recently, including the one occupied by Andrew Grove, Intel's chairman and chief executive.

9 "It was done to maintain the consistency of egalitarian standards," said Patricia Murray, vice president for human resources. "If the rank-and-file has to do with less temporarily, so do the executives. There's no mahogany row at Intel."

10 Microsoft's corporate campus in suburban Seattle, on the other hand, is inhabited by unrepentant "cave" dwellers. The company's bias toward private offices stems from the belief of its founders, Bill Gates and Paul Allen, that software programmers work best in the solitude of individual offices.

11 "Every time we revisit the issue of having open-plan offices, it is roundly rejected," said Nick MacPhee, Microsoft's general manager of real estate and facilities. "The reaction borders between horror and hysteria."

12 Yet the open-plan office—ranging from Mr. Rouady's quirky digs, spanned by a replica of the Golden Gate Bridge built with soda cans, to the look-alike cubicles satirized in the cartoon strip Dilbert—continues to march through corporate America. An estimated 40 million Americans, nearly 60 percent of the white-collar work force, now work in cubes.

13 The cubist ranks are growing, according to surveys by the International Facility Management Association, a trade group for office planners and designers.

14 One of the bastions of closed-office culture, International Business Machines Corp., will fall next month when it opens its new headquarters in Armonk, New York, which is to be more than 90 percent open-plan.

Office Gossip: Which Is Better?

Is your office a "cube" in a large communal space or a "cave" that affords privacy? Proponents of each hold strong views about which is best-suited for doing business. Here are some arguments for each style.

CAVE		CUBE
Real work requires real thinking. And an office is the place to think.	Productivity	Offices are for wimps. Even Intel's Andy ("Only the Paranoid Survive") Grove works in a cube.
If you want to talk to someone, you can go find the person. Or try the phone or E-mail.	Communication	A real advantage for cubes. Just stand up and wave your hands to attract attention. Or shout.
An office and a door says you're someone special.	Status	Anybody who needs an office for status is pathetic.
We respect an individual's privacy.	Corporate Culture	We have a culture of trust and our workers actually like each other.
A person's office is his or her castle, as tasteful or tacky as its occupant.	Design	Workers must respect the sensibilities of others, but also allow for group design projects.
Great for gossiping and intimate conversations.	Socializing	Great for overhearing gossip fodder. It's the 90s: no intimate chat on company time.

N.Y. Times News Service

15 There is some evidence of a softening of positions on both sides of the cave-cube divide. Eric Richert, director of workplace effectiveness at a private-office stronghold, Sun Microsystems, is participating in an office-sharing experiment to open up more team-meeting space.

16 "We're trying not to take a religious approach to the workspace issue," he said.

17 In any case, offices of all kinds are shrinking. The Facility Performance Group, a research firm, says personal work space has shrunk 25 percent to 50 percent over the past decade at 72 major companies it has studied.

18 The office downsizing is partly a result of cost cuts. But most of these companies have also gone through "re-engineering" programs intended to replace traditional hierarchies with teamwork in the pursuit of greater innovation, speed and profits.

19 A shift to open-plan offices is often part of the re-engineering formula. With the cubes come more team-meeting rooms, so personal space is sacrificed. Cubists insist their approach is a winner.

20 "All the accepted research in this field says you have to have more visual and acoustic openness to get the benefits of a team-based organization," said Jon Ryburg, president of Facility Performance Group in Ann Arbor, Michigan.

21 Perhaps that's true for an automaker or an insurance company, the cave dwellers reply, but a different set of work-space principles prevails on the frontiers of the new economy.

22 "People who have to think deeply, like programmers, need individual offices," said Eric Schmidt, the former chief technology officer for Sun Microsystems Inc., who recently became chairman of Novell Inc., a software company. "The best and the brightest drive this industry and the high-tech economy. Giving them an office to

be more productive is a smart investment."

23 This is the cavers' trump card: Programmers are special people who do special work. They must cooperate with others at times, but theirs is essentially individual labor—hours of tedious, painstaking effort punctuated by flashes of inspiration, all rendered in the arcane language of machines.

24 People who study how programmers work speak of cognitive "flow," the code cowboy's equivalent of an athlete being in a peak-performance "zone" when everything seems to work. Deep concentration helps the code flow, and that mental state, many programmers say, is easier to attain in a private office.

25 Besides, they add, private offices proved to be a recruiting advantage in Silicon Valley's earlier boom in the late 1980s: At that time, Sun had just expanded, building many private offices—and helping to lure many job candidates.

I. Getting the Message

A. Reading for Main Ideas

After reading the article, circle the best answer for each item.

1. The main purpose of this article is to
   a. argue that offices are better than cubicles.
   b. show that closed-in offices are becoming increasingly popular.
   c. describe a major disagreement about office design.

2. Cubicles are a big part of
   a. an "open-plan layout."
   b. "closed-office culture."
   c. the "old-line hierarchy."

3. Bill Gates and Paul Allen, founders of Microsoft, are in favor of
   a. closed-in offices.
   b. open offices.
   c. a mixture of closed and open office spaces.

4. Most American office workers now work
   a. in cubicles.
   b. in offices.
   c. at home.

5. Currently, the size of both private offices and cubicles is
   a. getting bigger.
   b. getting smaller.
   c. not changing significantly.

6. One advantage the "caves" may actually have today is that they may
   a. promote easy exchange of ideas.
   b. help in getting people to join a company.
   c. be better for use of computer networks and e-mail.

Check your answers with the key on page 117. If you have made mistakes, reread the article to gain a better understanding of it.

B. Understanding Ideas

This article describes a "debate" between those who favor cubicles, "cubes," and those who favor private offices, "caves." In this exercise read each statement, and then write "cube" or "cave" next to it, depending on which side is likely to make such a statement.

1. _____ Computer programmers need to work alone to be creative.

2. _____ Openness is necessary for teamwork.

3. _____ People work best when they feel equal.

4. _____ Workers need to respect and understand the power of the boss.

5. _____ Workers need to feel respected and special.

6. _____ Everyone must work together to be as productive as possible.

II. Expanding Your Vocabulary

A. Getting Meaning from Context

Find each word in the paragraph indicated in parentheses. Use context clues to determine the meaning of the word. Choose the definition that fits the context.

1. partitions (2)	a. desks	b. low walls
2. seamlessly (3)	a. smoothly	b. without discussion
3. contentious (4)	a. causing argument	b. not very important
4. splits (6)	a. creates	b. divides
5. stance (7)	a. opinion	b. way in which someone stands
6. unrepentant (10)	a. not sorry	b. not repeating
7. shift (19)	a. change	b. group of workers
8. tedious (23)	a. boring	b. exciting
9. punctuated (23)	a. on time	b. interrupted
10. lure (25)	a. attract	b. reject

Study the meanings of these idioms and expressions. A form of each one appears in the indicated paragraph of the article.

vie with (headline) be in competition with

software programmer (1) a person who writes software for computers

programming code (3) the special language that enables a computer program to work

rank-and-file (9) ordinary members, not the leadership

mahogany row (9) the fancy offices of the upper-level executives, which sometimes have costly wood paneling and furniture

bastion will fall (14) the last protection of something will finally be defeated; a *bastion* refers to a place that is strongly fortified or protected

in any case (17) anyhow; no matter what was just said

office downsizing (18) the reduction in the size of an office and the individual worker's space

go through (18) experience

the best and the brightest (22) the most able and intelligent young workers

Complete these sentences, using the idioms and expressions.

1. Intel and Microsoft have a disagreement about the kind of office that a

   _____ needs to do one's best work.

2. The _____, not the top executives, are the ones who usually

   worry about downsizing and layoffs on their jobs.

3. If companies want to hire _____, they need to research carefully

   the office conditions that workers find attractive.

4. Most office workers do not like to give up working space because of an

   _____. Every inch of personal space a worker has is highly valued.

IV. Making Sense of Sentences

The usual question pattern in English is *helping verb—subject—main verb.*

> **Example:** Why ***do*** <u>you</u> **favor** cubicles? (*Do* is the helping verb; *you* is the subject; *favor* is the main verb.)

But when the question word is the subject of the verb, statement word order is used.

> **Examples:** <u>Who</u> **favors** traditional offices? (*Who* is the subject; *favors* is the main verb.)
>
> <u>What</u> ***is*** **causing** office downsizing? (*What* is the subject; *is* is the helping verb; *causing* is the main verb.)

Imagine that you are the journalist interviewing people for this article. What questions would you ask each person to get the information or quotation from these paragraphs?

1. Bill Rouady, paragraph 1: **What are the essential ingredients of success for a**

   computer programmer?

2. Bill Rouady, paragraph 3: _____

3. Jon Ryburg, paragraph 20: _____

4. Eric Schmidt, paragraph 22 (first quotation): _____

5. Eric Schmidt, paragraph 22 (second quotation): _____

V. Talking and Writing

Discuss the following topics. Then choose one of them to write about.

1. If you could design your own ideal office space, how would you do it? Would it have "cubes" or "caves," or would it be very different? Describe it.

2. Look at the chart that goes with the article. Think about the side you favor. Which arguments for "your side" do you think are effective? Which arguments are not so effective? Do you have any other arguments to support your side?

3. What other ways is office work changing? How is each of these innovations—*e-mail, Internet, modems, telecommuting, laptop computers, faxes, office sharing, hoteling*—affecting office work?

2. *L'Air de* Jordan: Be like Mike, Smell like Mike

Previewing the Article

People want to look like Mike: they wear his brand of athletic shoes. They want to drive like Mike: they buy the sport utility vehicle he endorses. They even want to eat and drink like Mike: they eat the cereal and drink the sports drink he advertises. But do people want to smell like Mike? Of course, the Mike in question is Michael Jordan, the famous basketball player and one of the best-known people in the world.

This article is about a new Michael Jordan cologne that is entering into the competitive fragrance market. The humor of the piece rests on the contrast between the image of an adored but often very sweaty athlete and the elegant images typically associated with perfume advertising. The marketers of the new fragrance have faith, however, in the image of Jordan, who has successfully sold many products. In 1996 Jordan was reported to have made more than $40 million in product endorsements—in addition to his salary of $30 million playing for the Chicago Bulls. Since the introduction of his fragrance, Jordan has also come out with his own line of athletic clothing and shoes.

The following information will help you read the article with greater understanding:

- *Brad Pitt, Isabella Rossellini,* and *Elizabeth Taylor* are well-known actors.
- *Gabriela Sabatini* is an Argentinian tennis player who has her own line of fragrances.
- *Mike Ditka* is a football coach, formerly the coach of the Chicago Bears.
- *Bill Blass* and *Gianni Versace* are famous brand names in the fashion industry.
- *Michael Jordan* grew up in North Carolina and played basketball there. In 1996 he starred in a movie with the animated cartoon character Bugs Bunny.

Before You Read

Discuss these questions.

1. What do you know about Michael Jordan, of the Chicago Bulls, and the quality of his basketball playing? Have you watched him play basketball on television?

2. Some fragrances begin with the French words *L'air de* . . . meaning "the aroma of" or "aura of." Michael Jordan is often called "Air Jordan," because of his ability to jump high into the air to score baskets. There is a famous television commercial for a sports drink that tells the audience to drink the product and "Be like Mike." Can you explain the humor of the headline?

As You Read

Look for two reasons that Michael Jordan's cologne is different from previous product endorsements he has made.

L'Air de Jordan: Be like Mike, Smell like Mike

By Richard Sandomir
New York Times Service

1   You don't only take a quick whiff. You savor this fragrance. You let it invade your sinuses. Groove on the scent . . . So light. So refreshing. It will not precede you into a room like a noxious cloud.

2   The name behind it? Brad Pitt? No. Isabella Rossellini? No. Think of a tall man in a tank top, baggy shorts and sneakers who sweats for a living, a man who can more easily walk on a movie set with Bugs Bunny than on city streets with his public.

3   You've already tried to score, soar, dribble, drink and *be* like Mike?

4   You want to smell like him, too? Smell the way he does, not drenched and gamy after 50 points, but the way you imagine he does after $50 MILLION?

5   Just when you thought he was over-marketed and overexposed, Michael Jordan is in the olfactory business, hawking Michael Jordan Cologne, which was introduced on Monday.

6   You can spray on the scents that define Mike and that he defines as the very essences of his zest for life: the lavender and juniper of golf fairways; the suede and clove evoked by baseball glove leather; the tropical, lemony soul of Costa Rica; and the crisp cypress and rosewood of North Carolina and the sandalwood sensuality of the private Mike.

7   A joke? Not at all. This is the further marketing of the Jordan persona away from sport and the first time that a product has carried his full name. In a venture between the sublime Chicago Bull and the men's retail clothing line Bijan has shipped mass quantities of the clear, scented Jordan "juice" in a flask-like bottle with a sneaker tread on the bottom to department stores and sporting goods chains.

8   So you want tube socks, a Yankee World Series cap *and* 1.7 ounces of $23 Michael Jordan Cologne Spray? Step right up. You want the $15 Jordan shower gel, $12 Jordan body soap and $12 Jordan deodorant? Wait till next year.

9   "Michael's got a great sense of fashion," said David Falk, his agent. "The cologne is unisex, sporty and will be around for a long, long time. It's him."

10   Bijan hopes to lure 16- to 34-year-old men, the most fervent Jordanaires, the ones most likely to buy his sneakers, his battery, his sports drink, his sunglasses,

Reuters/Gary C. Caskey/Archive Photos

Michael Jordan tells it all.

his hot dog and his cereal.

11   Yet Bijan thinks that market also harbors secret desires to be the off-court Mike, of the sleek, tailored, expensive suits and shaven bean.

12   The sweat-soaked Jordan—the one who does not smell like the cologne—is a stigma that Bijan fast breaks from.

13   "He *looks* incredible," said Brett Neubig, a Bijan Fragrances spokesman. And he does not mean in his warm-up suit.

14   Bijan wants Jordan to be the Elizabeth Taylor of men's fragrances—not the now-retired Gabriela Sabatini, whose Gabriela perfume is no Chanel No. 5.

15   "There are 60 to 70 new fragrances a year, and you need a strong personality to pull away," said Annette Green, president of the Fragrance Foundation. "Michael Jordan crosses a lot of lines. He may sweat, but he's a good-looking, well-dressed fashion maven. I buy this."

16   No less an authority on fragrance than Mike Ditka, another Chicago icon, expects the fragrant Jordan to succeed. In 1986 the former football coach had Iron Mike cologne.

17   "A refreshing smell with a hint of citrus," he said. "I have a half bottle left."

18   (Yes, you could have smelled like *that* Mike!)

19   Ditka said Jordan has assets Iron Mike did not: global recognition, large-scale distribution and national advertising.

20   "People say, 'Why?'" Ditka said. "I say, 'Why not?' He's got a name in a class with Bill Blass and Versace."

21   Still, you wonder whether the cologne and Bijan's $20 million ad campaign (the black silhouette of Jordan's head on a red background will be as familiar as scenes from his new animated movie, "Space Jam," which opens Friday) will coerce Jordan's fans to make the buying leap to cologne.

22   "He can tell me about sneakers, he can tell me about how to quench my thirst," said Marty Blackman, whose Blackman and Raber firm matches athletes with corporations.

23   "That's all credible. But his personal decision on an aftershave, I don't know. You have to question it."

24   Don't expect Gatorade to help Jordan market his cologne. Gatorade loves Mike but prefers its drinkers malodorous. So there will be no joint promotions with Bijan.

25   As P. J. Sinopoli, a Gatorade spokeswoman, said, "We want his fans to sweat and smell so bad they'll need Gatorade."

26   Well, Jordan will have deodorant next year.

I. Getting the Message

After reading the article, circle the best answer for each item.

1. Besides reporting about a new cologne with Michael Jordan's name on it, the article
   a. explains why marketers believe Jordan's name on a cologne will attract buyers.
   b. analyzes how celebrities make money in business.
   c. explains the popularity of fragrance products such as cologne and perfume.

2. The writer says that the reader may think the Jordan cologne is a joke because
   a. Michael Jordan is known for jokes.
   b. readers may not associate a basketball player with smelling good.
   c. Michael Jordan does not wear cologne.

3. People marketing Michael Jordan cologne expect it to be popular with
   a. young women and men.
   b. men under 34.
   c. people who exercise every day.

4. One sign that the fragrance business is highly competitive is that
   a. sports figures seldom endorse fragrances.
   b. Jordan's cologne is $23 for 1.7 ounces.
   c. 60 to 70 new fragrances are introduced each year.

5. Mike Ditka, a sports figure who himself once had a cologne named after him, thinks that Michael Jordan Cologne will
   a. fail because his own was not very popular.
   b. succeed because of Michael's immense popularity.
   c. fail because Michael is an athlete, not a fashion model.

Check your answers with the key on page 117. If you have made mistakes, reread the article to gain a better understanding of it.

II. Expanding Your Vocabulary

A. Getting Meaning from Context

Find each word in the paragraph indicated in parentheses. Use context clues to determine the meaning of the word. Choose the definition that fits the context.

1. savor (1)   a. remember   b. enjoy

2. noxious (1)   a. harmful   b. noisy

3. olfactory (5)   a. relating to factories b. relating to smell

4. zest (6)   a. excitement   b. thoughtfulness

5. evoked (6)   a. hidden   b. produced

6. stigma (12)   a. negative image   b. signal

7. icon (16)   a. sports figure   b. highly respected person

8. assets (19)   a. advantages   b. investments

B. Categorizing Words

Find the term that does *not* belong in each category.

1. the sense of smell: **whiff, fragrance, sinuses, scents, persona**

2. a cosmetic product: **sneakers, shower gel, body soap, deodorant, aftershave**

3. a food: **cereal, hot dog, fans, sports drinks**

4. a type of clothing: **tank top, sneakers, suits, battery**

5. related to basketball: **fast break, dribble, silhouette, score**

6. related to marketing: **ad campaign, promotions, hawking, fairways**

III. Working with Idioms and Expressions

Study the meanings of these idioms and expressions. A form of each one appears in the indicated paragraph of the article.

take a whiff (1) smell briefly and quickly

groove on (1) enjoy, a slang expression

fast break from (12) a quick move away, from a basketball term that means to move the ball away quickly from the opposing team's side to one's own basket

pull away (15) get ahead of competitors

fashion maven (15) fashion expert or leader

make the buying leap to (21) buy something different or new

Answer the following questions.

1. Why do people want to *take a whiff* of a cologne before they buy it?

2. How can a cologne *pull away* from its competition?

3. If Michael Jordan is a *fashion maven,* how does he dress?

4. If Jordan's fans buy his cologne, why can you say they are *making a buying leap*?

IV. Analyzing Paragraphs

Write the number of the paragraph or paragraphs that give the following information.

1. _____ The ingredients in Michael Jordan's cologne

2. _____ The kind of people the cologne company hopes will buy the product

3. _____ The kind of bottle in which the cologne is sold

4. _____ Other products in the Michael Jordan cologne line

5. _____ Products other than cologne that Michael Jordan endorses

6. _____ The opinion of a person in sports and business who questions whether people will buy Michael Jordan's cologne

7. _____ The opinion of a sports figure who thinks that the cologne will succeed

V. Talking and Writing

Discuss the following topics. Then choose one of them to write about.

1. Do you wear a fragrance, a cologne or perfume? Why did you choose it and not another one? Did advertising have anything to do with your choice?

2. Have you seen Michael Jordan in any of his television commercials or in the 1996 film *Space Jam*? What is appealing about his presence? Describe the way he looks and acts.

3. What other celebrities can you name who endorse various products in television commercials? Do you think celebrity endorsements are an effective way to market products? Why or why not? Do celebrity endorsements affect what you buy?

4. What is the most effective commercial or advertisement that you have seen lately? Why do you find it effective?

Focus on the Newspaper

The business section of a newspaper contains information that affects people's economic lives. Individuals with money to invest can find information and advice that will help them earn money on investments in stocks, bonds, or real estate. Everyone can find information about employment trends and developing career areas. Since the current economy is a global one, economic events in other countries can affect business everywhere, so these events are reported in newspapers.

Topics of Business Articles

You will find a variety of articles in the business section, including the following:

- articles reporting the financial situation of companies, whether they are running at a profit or a loss
- articles reporting new products and technology developed or being developed by businesses and how these might affect the businesses
- information on whether currencies, such as the dollar, are going up or down in value
- articles on how political policies and elections are affecting business

All the articles help readers understand current business conditions.

Exercise 1: It's Your Business

Analyze a business article by answering the questions in the box titled "Analyzing a Business Article."

Analyzing a Business Article

1. What is the headline? How does it help you predict the content and viewpoint of the article?

2. What is the purpose of the article? (to report conditions of a company, a new product, trends in the stock market, experts' opinions on economic conditions, and so on)

3. What is the main idea of the article?

4. Does the article make a prediction about the future? If so, what is the prediction?

5. Does the article give the reader any advice? If so, what is it?

BUSINESS

Exercise 2: The Language of Business

Like all areas, business uses its own special vocabulary. To understand business articles, you need to know terms such as *recession, bonds, stocks, futures,* and *bull market.* Read two or three articles from the business section of a newspaper. Write down at least five sentences that include business terms you don't know and underline the terms. Discuss the terms in class and see if you can define them. Research the meanings of any terms you can't define.

Exercise 3: How's Business?

Scan the newspaper business section for a few weeks to find information about general business conditions in your area. As you read, look for answers to the following questions. Be prepared to discuss your conclusions with the class.

1. Is it difficult to find a job right now? Why or why not? In what fields are employment opportunities best?

2. What are some good investment opportunities now, according to the experts?

3. What economic problems does your area face at this time?

4. What is the overall economic outlook—optimistic or pessimistic?

Reading Stock Prices

Daily newspapers run long lists of the stock and bond prices of companies on the major exchanges. Investors who own any of these stocks or bonds can follow the fluctuating prices in the daily paper.

Exercise 4: The Ups and Downs

In class, practice reading the newspaper listing of stock prices. (Note that some newspapers provide a key to help you read the information.) Then choose the stock of a well-known company on one of the major exchanges. "Purchase" one hundred shares and follow the closing price for any four days within a two-week period. At the end of the two weeks, "sell" the stock. During the period that you "own" the stock, record the following information:

Name of stock purchased _____

Date of purchase _____   **Price per share** _____

Date _____ Closing price _____   Date _____ Closing price _____

Date _____ Closing price _____   Date _____ Closing price _____

Profit or loss (on 100 shares) _____

Do you know any reasons that the price went up or down?

PROFILES

Focus on the Newspaper: Profiles

1. Mind Your Etiquette: The New Emily Post

Previewing the Article

For many people, the word *etiquette* calls to mind silly, unimportant questions such as "Which spoon should I use for the soup?" and "Should a man open a door for a woman?"

But for others, especially the authors of books on modern manners, etiquette is a serious topic. It involves issues of morality, fairness, kindness—issues that affect all the ways people interact with one another. One of these writers, Peggy Post, is the subject of this profile. She is the great-granddaughter-in-law of Emily Post, author of the most famous guide to manners, *Emily Post's Etiquette*. Since 1922 readers have turned to this book for guidance on manners, and this article is written on the occasion of Peggy Post's new edition of the book.

Of course, a book originally based on rules of behavior from the 1920s needs updating to meet the challenges of continually changing lifestyles. Today people are likely to ask questions about etiquette for the use of cellular phones and beepers. They also worry about offending friends of other religions at holiday time and whether to mention ex-spouses in wedding invitations.

Derived from a French word for "tickets," the word *etiquette* originally referred to posted rules of behavior at the royal court. Although modern life is vastly different from that aristocratic world, the concern with not offending others in social situations has not changed. As Emily Post once wrote, "Manners are a sensitive awareness of the feelings of others. If you have that awareness, you have good manners, no matter what fork you use."

These are two important etiquette writers referred to in the article:

- *Letitia Baldrige* is the author of *The Complete Guide to the New Manners of the '90's*. She was the White House social secretary to Jacqueline Kennedy in the 1960s.

- *Judith Martin* has written several books and writes the syndicated "Miss Manners" column in which she answers questions from readers. Her writing is known for its humor and irony.

Before You Read

Discuss these questions.

1. Have you ever consulted a book of etiquette to answer a question about social behavior? What was your question? Did you follow the advice in the book?

2. What situations have you faced in which you needed to know the "proper" thing to do? How did you find the answer?

As You Read

As you read, look for information about Peggy Post's revision of Emily Post's book. How would you describe the book?

Mind Your Etiquette: The New Emily Post

By Enid Nemy
New York Times Service

Norman Y. Lono/The New York Times

Peggy Post has revised her great-grandmother-in-law's guide.

1 NEW YORK—Who needs it? Not you! You know which fork to use when. You never crook your pinkie when holding a cup. And you're always on time for appointments. Etiquette? Get serious!

2 That attitude is likely to give a high priestess of manners a hissy fit. Most people, it seems, haven't a clue what etiquette means.

3 Etiquette, in the 1990s, is about niceties like not cutting off motorists when switching lanes, or not swatting anyone with your backpack on the subway. "Etiquette is a code of behavior based on consideration and thoughtfulness, and it's a fallacy that only certain people need it," said Peggy Post, a great-granddaughter-in-law of Emily Post, the doyenne of the etiquette gurus, who for almost eight decades has stood for what's proper in social behavior. Peggy Post has inherited the legacy: She has just updated "Emily Post's Etiquette" for the 75th-anniversary edition, which will be published by HarperCollins next month. "The whole thing about etiquette is to make life easier," Post said, "not to make it more formal or rigid. Everyone needs guidelines."

4 What is also needed before tackling the new volume, the 16th edition, is a session or two of strength training. The new dos and don'ts of making life easier take up 845 tightly packed pages. Is it O.K. to cut lettuce in a salad? Yes. (The taboo started because knives used to become corroded from salad dressing.) Brides should perk up at this one: there's no reason why the bridegroom shouldn't do his share of note writing, and many more now do.

5 On the subject of personal questions: How do you answer someone who asks your age, assuming you don't want to reveal it? Post—who acknowledges that some people think the question rude but says, "I'm in the middle"—advised answering with humor and offered some alternatives: "Old enough to know better," "49 and holding."

6 Her own age? "I'm starting this about the same age as Emily did," she said cagily. Emily Post was 51 in 1922 when her first etiquette guide, "Etiquette: The Blue Book of Social Usage," was published.

7 When she died in 1960, she had completely revised the book nine times. It is still, according to a spokesman for the 435 Barnes & Noble stores in the United States, the best-selling book in its category.

8 Reflecting the changes in society, Peggy Post's style is not quite as formal as Emily Post's, but neither is it as breezy or irreverent as many of the current crop of etiquette books. "This is a reference book," she said firmly.

9 Margaret (Peggy) Post, who was born in Washington, was a manager at Chemical Bank in New York when she met Allen Post, an investment counselor, in 1977.

10 "I was taken aback when I found out who he was," she recalled of their first dinner date, when a reference to another Emily prompted a mention of his great-grandmother. "But he was such a natural, down-to-earth person I didn't think about it." They married in 1979 and live in Fairfield County, Connecticut.

11 It wasn't until after raising two stepsons that she began her apprenticeship with the Emily Post Institute, the umbrella organization for the Emily Post franchise, which includes 13 books, a Good Housekeeping magazine column that has run for 25 years and etiquette lectures. Soon she was making appearances at bridal events with Elizabeth Post, her mother-in-law and Emily's granddaughter-in-law, who revised the book five times between 1965 and 1992. On Elizabeth's retirement in 1995, Peggy Post took over the Good Housekeeping column ("How do you eat a cherry tomato? Carefully!") and started working on the new edition of the book. Elizabeth Post's daughter and three sons were "not inclined" to take on their mother's work, Peggy Post said.

12 "I've tried to make it more multicultural, more relevant," she said. There are lists of holy days for Buddhists, Christians, Hindus, Muslims, Jehovah's Witnesses and Jews; suggestions on the legal aspects of living together and how single mothers might deal

with their children's questions on parentage; and advice on public displays of affection. ("Holding hands, affectionate greetings accompanied by a kiss on the cheek, or a quick hug, are perfectly acceptable in public. Passion is not.") And a sign of the times: the word "servant" is out. It's now staff member or housekeeper.

13   What to do when ethnic jokes are told? There's no need to laugh or silently support such a display of poor taste, Post writes. "You may quietly say: 'I don't support what you're saying' or 'I don't like jokes that belittle people,' or simply get up and take your leave."

> **'I'm starting this about the same age as Emily did,' Peggy Post said.**

14   Which brings up Judith Martin's theory that although there is still a long way to go, there has been a vast improvement in etiquette in this country since Emily Post's day. What's that again? This from the etiquette maven who wrote "Miss Manners Rescues Civilization" (Crown Publishers) and four other Miss Manners books? "Racism and sexism no longer meet with social approval," she explained. What have racism and sexism to do with etiquette? "Etiquette is for respect and dignity," she said. "It is human social behavior."

15   And what about the general state of manners? Serious and alarming are two of the words used, but Post, Martin and Letitia Baldrige, who has seven etiquette books under her belt, maintain nevertheless that the pendulum is swinging.

16   Martin points out that more than a generation ago society went through a phase of deploring anything artificial and asked, Why can't people just behave naturally? Then, the reaction was, "Everyone is so rude, so disgusting."

17   "The kids who got away with it now know better," Martin said, "and they're not going to let their children get away with it. I think etiquette is on the upswing."

18   Post concurred: "There's a lot of discussion about people being rude and uncivil. They now want some control over their lives." Sounding very much like Emily Post, she added, "They are looking for a sense of order."

I. Getting the Message

A. Reading for Key Ideas

After reading the article, indicate whether each statement is true (**T**) or false (**F**).

1. _____ Peggy Post believes that only some people need etiquette and that most people don't.

2. _____ Peggy Post believes that understanding the rules of etiquette makes social life easier.

3. _____ The new edition of *Emily Post's Etiquette* is very long.

4. _____ Peggy Post believes that it is always improper to ask an adult his or her age.

5. _____ Peggy Post writes a magazine column on the subject of etiquette.

6. _____ According to Peggy Post, short hugs and kisses are not appropriate in public.

7. _____ Judith Martin believes that manners are much worse today than they were in the 1920s.

8. _____ Peggy Post believes that etiquette is more popular and in demand today than it was more than a generation ago, when people wanted to act "naturally."

Check your answers with the key on page 117. If you have made mistakes, reread the article to gain a better understanding of it.

B. Reading for Details

In the course of the article, rules of etiquette are mentioned. Write **yes** or **no** on the line after the sentence to tell whether the rule follows what is given in Peggy Post's book. Write **not given** if a rule is not mentioned in the article.

1. It is OK for the groom to write thank-you notes after a wedding. _____

2. It is not OK to put your elbows on the table while eating. _____

3. It is not OK to use a knife to cut the lettuce in your salad. _____

4. It is OK to avoid answering questions about your age. _____

5. You should never express disapproval of an ethnic joke. _____

6. It is OK to shake hands when introduced. _____

7. It is not OK to hold hands in public. _____

8. It is OK to use the word *servant*. _____

9. You should not call people you don't know well after 10 o'clock. _____

10. You use forks beginning with the one farthest from the plate. _____

II. Expanding Your Vocabulary

Getting Meaning from Context

Find each word in the paragraph indicated in parentheses. Use context clues to determine the meaning of the word. Choose the definition that fits the context.

1. swatting (3)	a. pulling	b. hitting
2. doyenne (3)	a. the richest woman	b. the oldest woman
3. taboo (4)	a. a strict rule against something	b. a special salad fork
4. revised (7, 11)	a. rewrote	b. changed one's mind
5. breezy (8)	a. formal	b. lively
6. maven (14)	a. an expert	b. a follower
7. phase (16)	a. a period of time	b. a legal system
8. deploring (16)	a. supporting	b. criticizing

Study the meanings of these idioms and expressions. A form of each one appears in the indicated paragraph of the article.

crook one's pinkie (1) hold up the smallest finger of a hand while holding a cup

hissy fit (2) acting very upset over a small matter in an undignified way

cut off (3) steer one's car abruptly in front of another car without warning

dos and don'ts (4) rules that apply in a certain situation

perk up (4) suddenly become more lively and active

do one's share (4) do a proper amount of work so that others don't have to do extra work

be taken aback (10) be very surprised

sign of the times (12) an indication of the way people think today

take one's leave (13) walk away

bring up (14) start a discussion of a topic

get away with something (17) do something wrong but avoid punishment

on the upswing (17) becoming more popular

Complete these sentences, using the idioms and expressions.

1. Peggy Post believes that interest in etiquette is _____.

2. One _____ is that *Emily Post's Etiquette* contains lists of holy days for many different religious faiths.

3. All books on etiquette contain _____ for special occasions such as weddings and funerals.

4. Drivers who _____ other cars endanger people's lives.

IV. Focusing on Style and Tone

The lively and humorous tone of this article is established in part by the writer's use of *irony*. Whenever possible, the reporter points out aspects of the story that are unexpected or ironic. For example, in paragraph 2 the author imagines an etiquette writer—a supposedly dignified and calm person—having a "hissy fit" (a ridiculous exhibition of frustration) over bad manners.

In the following exercise, write **I** for *ironic* and **NI** for *not ironic* next to each statement.

1. (paragraph 3) Not cutting off a motorist and not hitting someone with a backpack are referred to as "niceties" of modern etiquette. _____

2. (paragraph 3) The great-granddaughter-in-law of Emily Post has written a new edition of Post's famous etiquette book. _____

3. (paragraph 4) After reporting that Peggy Post's goal is to show that etiquette makes life easier, the writer notes that Post's book is so heavy a reader may need strength training just to pick it up. _____

4. (paragraph 12) Peggy Post's revised edition of the famous etiquette book reflects basic changes in the way people live and think today. _____

5. (paragraph 14) Judith Martin, who wrote a book entitled *Miss Manners Rescues Civilization*, believes that people have better manners today than years ago. _____

6. (paragraph 18) Peggy Post sounds very much like Emily Post. _____

V. Talking and Writing

Discuss the following topics. Then choose one of them to write about.

1. An interesting question asked in this article is whether manners are generally getting better or getting worse. What do you think? What examples can you use to support your idea?

2. Have you ever been angered or irritated by what you considered to be the rude behavior of others? Write an imaginary letter to an etiquette newspaper columnist about your complaint. Then write the columnist's answer.

3. Have you ever been in a social situation in which your idea of what was acceptable differed from that of others? What was the situation? What were the differences?

4. Rules of good behavior can be different in different countries and cultures. Have you ever experienced any such differences? What were they?

2. Henny Youngman, King of the One-Liners, Dies

Previewing the Article

Are you a fan of stand-up comedy? In this style of humor, a comedian stands alone on a stage and tells *one-liners,* which are very brief jokes told very quickly. If you enjoy Jay Leno or David Letterman on late-night TV in the United States, you are familiar with this comedic style.

One of the all-time masters of this form is the subject of this profile, the comedian Henny Youngman. Youngman, who died in 1998, had a career that spanned the 20th century. His long career reveals much about the history of entertainment in the United States. He started in the business at the beginning of the century in *vaudeville,* which was the principal form of entertainment in the United States from the 1880s into the 1930s. A vaudeville show featured a wide variety of live acts—jugglers, singers, animal acts, magicians, and comics.

Youngman also worked in the *Borscht Belt,* an area in the Catskill Mountains west of the Hudson River in upstate New York. The area's many resort hotels are famous for presenting the stand-up comedy of Jewish comedians. Current well-known comedians such as Woody Allen, Jerry Seinfeld, Paul Reiser, Billy Crystal, and Gary Shandling have extended the Borscht Belt tradition into television situation comedy and films.

Here are facts about two important comedians mentioned in the article:

- *Milton Berle* was a famous comedian during the early days of television. His *Texaco Star Theater* (1948–1956) sometimes captured 80 percent of the television audience.
- *Jack Benny* (1894–1974) had an enormously successful career in radio, television, and films. His humor centered on his reluctance to spend money and to admit his age: he eternally remained 39 years old.

Before You Read

Discuss these questions.

1. Do you know of any stand-up comedians? What do these comedians have in common? What differences in style do they show?

2. Henny Youngman's most famous one-liner is "Take my wife—please!" This joke relies on two meanings for the word *take*. What are they? Why is this joke so funny?

As You Read

As you read, find out why people typically picture Henny Youngman with a violin in his hand.

Henny Youngman, King of the One-Liners, Dies

By Mervyn Rothstein
New York Times Service

1 NEW YORK—Henny Youngman, 91, the King of the One-Liners, who implored his audiences for more than six decades to "take my wife—please," died Tuesday in New York.

2 Youngman had been hospitalized since Jan. 2. He had come down with a cold while on a two-show-a-night visit to San Francisco the week after Christmas. Back in New York, it developed into pneumonia.

3 The most rapid-fire of rapid-fire comics, he could tell six, seven, sometimes even eight or more jokes a minute, 50 or more jokes in an eight-minute routine. Rarely if ever did a joke last more than 24 seconds.

4 For Youngman, every good joke was "really a simple cartoon—you can SEE it," he wrote in his 1991 autobiography, "Take My Life, Please!"

5 "A man says to another man, 'Can you tell me how to get to Central Park?' The guy says no. 'All right,' says the first, 'I'll mug you here.' Two guys are in a gym, and one is putting on a girdle. 'Since when have you been wearing a girdle?' says his friend. 'Since my wife found it in the glove compartment of our car.'"

6 For much of his career, Youngman would travel a half million miles or more a year in the United States and Canada, appearing in more than 100 engagements at nightclubs in Las Vegas, Los Angeles, Montreal, Chicago and New York, at sales meetings, colleges, synagogues, banquets and hotels, cruises to Mexico and the West Indies, on television variety shows and in guest stints with Johnny Carson, Ed Sullivan, Merv Griffin or whoever else would have him. "I can go anywhere, play any date, for any kind of people," Youngman said.

7 He was not happy unless he got at least 10 bookings a month, 10 opportunities to place his stocky 6-foot-2 frame on a podium, brandish the 19th-century violin that he had taken to calling a "Stradivaricose," and make people laugh.

8 Youngman was born March 16, 1906, in London, where he was named Henry Youngman. ("I was so ugly when I was born," he later said, "the doctor slapped my mother.")

9 His father, Yonkel Youngman, a hatmaker, had emigrated from Russia to Paris, then to London and then to the Lower East Side of New York, where, his name changed to Jacob Youngman, he met another immigrant, Olga Chetkin. The two married and went for their honeymoon to London, where Jacob's parents lived. They stayed for a year and a half—during which time Henry was born—until they finally earned enough money to return to the United States.

10 Back in New York, the Youngmans lived in a tenement owned by Henry's uncle.

11 His father, then a sign painter, loved music, especially opera. Henry's aunt bought him a violin, and his father decided he should become a violinist in the Metropolitan Opera orchestra.

12 During his high school days, Henry spent most of his time at vaudeville houses in the neighborhood—the Orpheum, the Fox, the Flatbush, the Prospect. He tried out the jokes he had heard in the theaters on friends in a neighborhood candy store. He also played his violin in the orchestra pit of a local movie house—the orchestra consisted only of Henny and a woman playing the piano.

13 He was known as Hen until age 18, when a headline in Bill-

The Associated Press

Henny Youngman with his "Stradivaricose" in 1983.

board read, "Hen Youngman and Syncopators Play Coney Island Boardwalk." Seeing his first mention in the newspaper, he decided that "hens lay eggs" and became Henny.

14 He got jobs serving summonses, at 50 cents apiece, and printing business cards at Kresge's department store in downtown Brooklyn. Across the aisle at Kresge's was a red-haired young woman selling sheet music named Sadie Cohen; she would become his wife of 58 years.

15 A quiet, almost anonymous woman, she allowed him to tell jokes about her, jokes that became his trademark: "I miss my wife's cooking—as often as I can"; "How's your wife?" "Compared to what?"; "I take my wife everywhere, but she always finds her way home."

16 "She took it with a grain of salt," Youngman said after his wife's death in 1987 at age 82. "She knew I was just joking. She always stuck by me, and that's what counts."

17 The young Henny's band eventually went to the Catskills, the Borscht Belt—the proving ground for so many Jewish comedians and singers.

18 Henny met a comedian who was headlining down the block at the Loew's State—Milton Berle. They became friends, and in the early years Berle would give him any jobs he didn't have time for. The change from musician to comedian came one night at the Nut Club in Mountainside, New Jersey, when the comedy team of Grace and Paul Hartman didn't show up for their performance.

Desperate, the manager asked Henny to go on for them. He was a hit—and, as a colleague later said, "Music's loss was comedy's loss."

19 He played clubs and speakeasies all over the East Coast. His performances, at least according to his jokes, were not always successes: "I won't say business was bad at the last place I played, but the band was playing 'Tea for One'"; "Fellow called up and said, 'What time is the next show?' I said, 'What time can you make it?'"

20 Youngman's first big break came in 1937 when he was signed for a six-minute spot on the Kate Smith radio show. He got so many laughs, he was kept on for 10 minutes. After the show, he was made a regular.

21 "I was a greenhorn," he recalled in his autobiography, written with Neal Karlen. "I came out of left field. I didn't even know enough to copy anybody. I wasn't trained. I wasn't taught. But overnight I became a star, so I had to learn the business. I got $250 for that first show. When I got home, my mother said, 'Since when have you been funny?' I showed her the check—and that's what convinced her I was funny."

22 And even though Jack Benny got there first, it was on the Kate Smith show that he first made his violin an important part of his act, alternating his rapid-fire jokes with terrible playing, often a phrase of "Smoke Gets in Your Eyes."

23 His most famous line, "Take my wife—please," was born by accident, when he used the phrase to ask a stagehand to show his wife and her friends to their seats before a radio program. "They were all talking and giggling while I was trying to read my script," he recalled. "Finally, I couldn't take it anymore. I took Sadie by the elbow and brought her over to a stagehand. 'Take my wife,' I said to the guy. 'PLEASE.'"

24 The secret of his lasting success in show business, he said, could be summed up in one Yiddish phrase: "Nem di gelt."

25 "Get the money," he explained in his autobiography. "Don't believe all the baloney people tell you when they're describing what they're going to do for you someday soon. Nem di gelt."

26 Even in his difficult final years, Youngman retained his sense of humor. At age 89, he broke his hip. Several months after leaving the hospital, he attended a celebration honoring his 90th birthday. His first quip? "Take my wheelchair—please."

I. Getting the Message

After reading the article, circle the best answer for each item.

1. At the time of his death, Henny Youngman
   a. had retired and was no longer working.
   b. was still performing.
   c. was known mainly as a violinist.

2. Henny Youngman was known as the King of the One-Liners because
   a. he was a good storyteller.
   b. he could tell many jokes very fast.
   c. he wrote one-liners for other comedians.

3. His father wanted Youngman to be a
   a. rabbi.
   b. surgeon.
   c. musician.

4. Youngman became a comedian
   a. when he saw Jack Benny's act.
   b. when he went onstage to replace a comedy act.
   c. because he wasn't making enough money as a musician.

5. The article suggests that Youngman was

    a. hardworking and funny.

    b. bitter about not being more famous.

    c. rich but not a very good comedian.

Check your answers with the key on page 117. If you have made mistakes, reread the article to gain a better understanding of it.

II. Expanding Your Vocabulary

A. Getting Meaning from Context

Find each word in the paragraph indicated in parentheses. Use context clues to determine the meaning of the word. Choose the definition that fits the context.

1. implored (1)	a. ordered	b. asked
2. routine (3)	a. something that is repeated	b. something that is funny
3. engagements (6)	a. agreements to marry	b. agreements to perform onstage
4. stocky (7)	a. heavy	b. slender
5. brandish (7)	a. wave something	b. name something
6. emigrated (9)	a. moved to a country	b. moved out of a country
7. giggling (23)	a. smiling widely	b. laughing quietly
8. baloney (25)	a. lunch meat	b. lies, untruths

B. Understanding the Language of Jokes

Answer these questions.

1. Reread the first joke in paragraph 5. The *punch line* (the funny final statement in a joke) is spoken by a thief: "I'll *mug* you here." To *mug* someone means to rob someone on the street. What comment does the joke make about Central Park in New York City?

2. Reread paragraph 7. A *Stradivarius* is an extremely rare and valuable violin made by the Italian violin maker Antonio Stradivarius (1644–1737) or his family. *Varicose veins* refers to a medical condition sometimes associated with older people. What does Henny Youngman mean by calling his violin a "Stradivaricose"?

3. The first joke in paragraph 15 depends on two meanings of the word *miss*. What are the two meanings of the word? What does the joke mean?

4. A typical set phrase in English is "(Someone's) loss was my gain." What is the meaning of the line "Music's loss was comedy's loss" in paragraph 18? How does this show that Youngman was able to make fun of himself?

III. Working with Idioms and Expressions

Study the meanings of these idioms and expressions. A form of each one appears in the indicated paragraph of the article.

come down with (2) become ill

guest stints (6) brief appearances by a guest performer on a TV or radio show

play a date (6) keep an appointment to perform

try out (12) do something for the first time to test one's ability

with a grain of salt (16) not taken seriously or in an offended way

stick by someone (16) be loyal to someone

show up (18) appear for an appointment

first big break (20) the first important career opportunity

get laughs (20) cause an audience to laugh

greenhorn (21) a young person who doesn't know much

come out of left field (21) appear unexpectedly

Since when . . . ? (5, 21) the beginning of a question: "When did this surprising activity start?"

Complete these sentences, using the idioms and expressions. Use the correct forms of the verbs.

1. Even though Youngman constantly joked about his marriage, his wife always took

   the joking _____.

2. When Youngman started out in show business, he was a _____.

3. When Henny was very young, he often _____ his jokes on his

   friends.

4. Most Americans know about Henny Youngman because of his

   _____ on late-night television shows.

IV. Analyzing Paragraphs

Answer these questions about the article.

1. Paragraphs 6–7 describe Youngman's typical working schedule. What do these paragraphs suggest about his attitude toward his work?

    a. Youngman became exhausted traveling so much.

    b. Youngman loved his work and loved to travel.

2. Paragraphs 9–11 explain Youngman's family background. What do they show?

    a. Youngman's family wasn't rich, but it had musical ambitions for Henny.

    b. Youngman's father worked part-time as a musician, and he wanted his son to become one too.

3. Paragraphs 14–16 describe Youngman's wife. Which statement best describes his marriage?

    a. Although not much is publicly known about his wife, the marriage seemed happy.

    b. His marriage was troubled because of his constant jokes about his wife.

4. Paragraphs 20–21 describe how Youngman started to become well known as a comedian. Which statement describes his own reaction to his success?

    a. Youngman expected success because he had worked so hard at his craft.

    b. Youngman was surprised at his success because he was so inexperienced.

5. Paragraphs 24–25 describe Youngman's secret for success: "Get the money." What does this expression mean?

    a. Don't be fooled by show business people who make big promises.

    b. Don't do any charity performances without getting paid for them.

V. Talking and Writing

Discuss the following topics. Then choose one of them to write about.

1. There are many styles of humor. Some people in the United States would find Henny Youngman's jokes old-fashioned. What styles of humor are popular with people in your age group? What styles of humor are popular with people in other cultures you know?

2. What makes you laugh? What kind of comedy entertainment do you find the most amusing? Is it TV comedy shows? Is it certain kinds of comedy films, such as romantic comedies? Is it physical humor? Is it humor that is clever and relies on wordplay and puns? Describe some of your favorite examples of comedy.

3. Henny Youngman's father tried to influence his choice of career. Later, Henny became a comedian when by chance he replaced a comedy act. How do you think most people you know choose their careers? What is the role of their parents? What is the role of chance?

Focus on the Newspaper

The public is curious about people in the news. Whether these people are viewed as admirable or despicable, newspaper readers want to know all about them. A feature story that describes a person's lifestyle and attitudes is called a *profile*.

Some people are so prominent that they are always newsworthy. But most celebrity profiles are printed around the time of a news event involving that person. For example, a well-known entertainer is profiled when appearing in a new show; a famous athlete is profiled after winning a big game; and political figures are profiled near election time. A person who is not a celebrity may also be the subject of a profile if he or she has done something heroic or has been involved in an interesting story.

The Subjects of Profiles

Profiles in newspapers typically do the following: (1) tell something about a person's personal life; (2) tell about the person's current work or production; (3) reveal the person's professional goals, style, sources of inspiration, and attitudes toward his or her career.

The information in a profile comes from a journalist's interview with the person. A profile usually contains many direct quotations so that readers may share the experience of "hearing" the subject of the profile. A good profile makes readers feel that they know and understand the person being interviewed.

Exercise 1: What's in a Profile?

Find a profile in a newspaper. Analyze the article by answering the questions in the box titled "Analyzing a Profile."

Analyzing a Profile

1. Why did the newspaper run a profile on this person at this time?

2. Did you know anything about the person before you read the article? If so, did the article cause you to change your attitude toward this person? Did you find out anything that surprised you?

3. Did the article stimulate your interest in the person's work? Why or why not?

4. How does the author of the profile seem to feel toward the subject?

5. What influenced your impression of the subject the most: the quotations from the person being profiled or the comments of the writer of the profile?

6. What would you like to know about the subject that the article did not tell you?

How Profiles Personalize the News

Like other feature stories, profiles make newspaper (and magazine) reading more interesting. They tie events to the people who are involved in them. By comparing a news story with a profile, you will discover elements of style and content that enable a profile to draw a clear picture of a person in the news.

Exercise 2: Comparing a News Story and a Profile

In current issues of newspapers, find a news story and then a profile of a person involved in the news story. Compare the two articles. Put a check (✓) in the correct column to show which articles contained the following information.

Information	News Story	Profile
1. the subject's age	_____	_____
2. the subject's marital status	_____	_____
3. a physical description of the subject	_____	_____
4. information about the subject's education or childhood	_____	_____
5. a direct quotation of the subject's words	_____	_____
6. information about the subject's future plans	_____	_____
7. information about a controversy involving the subject	_____	_____
8. the journalist's attitude toward the subject	_____	_____
9. the reason for which the person is in the news now	_____	_____
10. clues or direct statements indicating that the journalist interviewed the subject face-to-face or over the phone	_____	_____
11. answers to the five "W" questions (who, what, when, where, why)	_____	_____

How to Write a Profile

Writing a good profile takes both skill and creativity. To find out how such a piece is put together, try writing one yourself. Follow these steps:

1. *Plan for the interview.* A good profile begins long before you sit down to write it. First, you must select an interesting subject—a person who is unusual in some way or who has had an unusual experience. Your subject must be accessible by phone or in person because it's difficult to write a good profile from secondary sources. You need an interview. Before the interview write a list of questions. Good questions bring out not only the facts of the person's life but also the person's values, opinions, and goals.

2. *Conduct the interview.* Go to the interview with a notepad, several pens or pencils, and (if possible) a tape recorder. Ask the subject's permission before taping. It's fine to adopt a conversational tone, but be sure that the subject, not you, does most of the talking. Include in your notes some of the subject's exact words so that you can quote the person directly. What does your subject look like? Take some notes on that. Also, if you are doing the interview in the subject's home or office, take notes on the surroundings, especially those that reveal something about the person's interests and habits.

3. *Write the profile.* Make the first paragraph an attention getter. Start with an anecdote, a surprising fact, or a direct quotation. Use at least two direct quotes in the piece. Include a description of the subject's physical appearance. After you finish your story, give it a headline and a dateline—and don't forget to give yourself a byline.

ARTS/ ENTERTAINMENT

Focus on the Newspaper: Arts / Entertainment

1. 'Noble' Laureate I. B. Singer: The Ultimate Typo

Previewing the Article

The word *typo* is short for "typographical error." It refers to a small mistake at the keyboard, such as typing "teh" instead of "the." But as all students know, these "small" mistakes can be a serious problem for someone seeking a good grade on a term paper. And in the world of business and law, a typo can mean the loss of large amounts of money. In this article a typo has emotional significance for people, for it was carved into the gravestone of a famous writer, Isaac Bashevis Singer.

Singer won the Nobel Prize for literature in 1978, and like other winners of this prestigious award, he was called a "Nobel laureate." A monument company spelled *Nobel* on the gravestone as the adjective *Noble*. Since both words describe Singer, the mistake looks like a pun, a joke based on two different meanings of a word. Of course, a pun on a gravestone seems in terribly bad taste. The mistake resulted in problems for Singer's family and an irritation for all who admire Singer's books and respect his memory.

Singer (1904–1991) was born in Poland and immigrated to the United States in 1935. He wrote almost entirely in Yiddish, the language of Jewish people in Eastern Europe. His writings were mainly about the life of people in the small Jewish towns in Eastern Europe, called *shtetl*, and Polish immigrant life in the United States. His work combines realism and the mysticism of Jewish folklore in a unique and memorable way.

Before You Read

Discuss these questions.

1. Look at the "before and after" picture of the gravestone. What differences do you see?

2. Why is this mistake called the "ultimate" typo in the headline? What are the meanings of *ultimate*? Why is the word used as a pun in the headline?

3. Have you ever read anything by Singer? If so, what are some of the characteristics of a Singer story?

As You Read

As you read, find out who was originally responsible for the mistake in Singer's gravestone.

'Noble' Laureate I. B. Singer: The Ultimate Typo

By Elisabeth Bumiller
New York Times Service

Liana Miuccio/The New York Times

Original epitaph on the stone at the foot of Singer's grave and correct version.

1   NEW YORK—What writer has not suffered the indignity of a typo? But for Isaac Bashevis Singer, this particular typo was the ultimate indignity: It was on his gravestone.

2   To some of his friends it was a cruel insult, a mistake set in stone. Others saw it as a comic absurdity, one that would have certainly been appreciated by Singer himself. His widow, like an antic Singer character afloat in her own world, was willing to let it pass.

3   But Wednesday, nearly six years after the death of the Yiddish writer who won the 1978 Nobel Prize for Literature, a monument engraver finally corrected Singer's honorific. Singer at last is a "Nobel" laureate, and no longer a "Noble" one, as his stone has proclaimed since 1992.

4   "Isaac would have enjoyed the irony," said Eve Friedman, the co-author with Singer of the play "Teibele and Her Demon." "But there was something kind of sad about it. Isaac in that stone was the butt of a joke."

5   The typo was one of several unfortunate leitmotifs in the tale surrounding Singer's final resting place. Another was his son's anger over the site of his father's grave: why did the author of "Gimpel the Fool," who wrote such farcical stories about the ambiguities of sex and death, end up buried in suburban New Jersey, in a casually kept grave site within view of an encroaching subdivision?

6   Yet another was the family's incredulity that Singer, who is described by his son as a "Jewish Casanova," was laid to rest three gravestones away from the man, Walter Wassermann, from whom he stole his second wife. That woman, Alma Singer, who died in 1996, now lies next to Singer, but within feet of Wassermann.

7   If this were a Singer short story ("The Re-encounter" comes to mind), Walter and Isaac would continue to glare at each other in death, through the yew bushes. "They hardly got along in life, so it's kind of ironic that they're neighbors in death," said Alma Singer's grandson, Stephen Dujack.

8   The typo was discovered in the summer of 1992 at the unveiling of the gravestone in Beth-El before family and friends.

9   Roger Straus, a founder of Farrar, Straus & Giroux, Singer's publisher, was horrified, and immediately pulled Mrs. Singer aside. "I said 'This is awful, what are we going to do?'" he recalled. Mrs. Singer responded, he said, that "Noble" was an "acceptable alternative."

10   The story begins in a Catskills resort. The then-Alma Wassermann, 30, a stylish, self-absorbed German-born refugee, was married to Walter Wassermann, a wealthy businessman. They had two young children. The family had recently fled Nazi Germany and settled in Manhattan. In the summer of 1937, they took their first American vacation at a farm in Mountaindale, New York. Nearby was Green Fields, a colony of Jewish writers, where Singer, 33, the son of a Warsaw rabbi and himself a recent immigrant, was staying.

11   Mrs. Wassermann and Singer became friends and went for long walks with her children. The relationship continued in the city, in clandestine meetings at the New York Public Library, and grew into a romance. By 1940, Wassermann had left her husband, as well as Inge, 10, and Klaus, 6, to marry Singer.

12   "I just felt that I had to spend the rest of my life with him, and therefore I had to give up my marriage and my children," Alma Singer later told Janet Hadda, the author of "Isaac Bashevis Singer: A Life."

13   Alma's daughter, Inge, never forgave her. Inge grew up, married Raymond Dujack, now an economist, and settled in the small New Jersey town of Emerson.

14   In 1964 Inge's father, Walter Wassermann, died. Inge, who had always loved the nearby Beth-El Cemetery, bought four plots near a tree, and buried her father in one. In 1990 Inge died of cancer at 60 and was buried in front of her father. Her mother, who by this time had been married for half a century to Singer, had not come to see her daughter during her illness. Inge was instead cared for by her friend and next-door neighbor, Leah Feingold.

15   The following year, Singer was dead. Mrs. Singer, searching for a suitable plot, called Feingold to help select a nice plot for Isaac. And one where there would be

room someday for her, too. "She said she wanted it as close to Inge as possible," Feingold said. "She had a lot of guilt about her daughter. A lot of guilt."

16 So Feingold found the grave for the Nobel laureate, just three stones away from Wassermann, Alma's ex-husband. "Alma didn't care about that," Feingold said.

17 At the unveiling the following year, the family found the "Noble" typo—and two others on the smaller footstone marking Singer's grave. There, Nobel was spelled wrong, and worse, at least in Mrs. Singer's view, the "h" had been dropped from her husband's middle name.

18 Mrs. Singer complained to Shastone Memorial Corp. in Great Neck, New York, the company that had made both gravestones. Shastone retorted that Mrs. Singer had specified both the "Noble" and "Basevis" spelling in her original instructions and produced documents showing her signed approval of blueprints of the stones, with all three mistakes.

19 After much mutual fingerpointing, Shastone replaced the footstone with a corrected one in June 1993, at a cost of $430 to the Singer family. "Noble" on the big stone stayed as it was.

20 In 1996, after Alma died, Susan Dujack, Alma's granddaughter, called a lawyer. Soon Shastone said they could make the change—for $625, which Israel Zamir would pay for—but not without the approval of the two other heirs, Steven Dujack, Alma's grandson, and Klaus Wassermann, Inge's brother. Wassermann quickly said yes, but Dujack balked. "Alma had chosen not to change it," Dujack said. "Why should I interfere with history? It had happened."

21 Dujack then spoke to Friedman, who reasoned with him, "Isaac," she told him, "would never want his dignity punctured to make a point about humanity."

22 That settled it. Wednesday in Beth-El, under an overcast sky, a monument engraver, Reed Frankel, knelt near the scruffy crab grass that edges Singer's grave, and carefully drilled away the past.

23 Would Singer be amused or annoyed by the fuss over his epitaph? A clue may lie in "The Reencounter." "Of all my disenchantments," a dead character says, "immortality is the greatest."

I. Getting the Message

After reading the article, indicate whether each statement is true (**T**) or false (**F**). For help reread the paragraphs indicated in parentheses.

1. _____ All of Singer's friends and relations felt angry about the typo. (2)

2. _____ The location of Singer's grave is unusual because it is close to that of his wife's ex-husband. (6, 7)

3. _____ Singer met and fell in love with his wife when she was married to someone else. (10, 11)

4. _____ Singer and his wife were married for more than 50 years. (14)

5. _____ On the small footstone marking Singer's grave, his name was spelled wrong. (17)

6. _____ Singer's family was able to prove that the mistakes were entirely the fault of the company that made the gravestone. (18)

7. _____ Because Singer was famous, his grave is more elaborate and better cared for than the graves of other people in the cemetery where he is buried. (5, 22)

Check your answers with the key on page 117. If you have made mistakes, reread the article to gain a better understanding of it.

II. Expanding Your Vocabulary

Getting Meaning from Context

Find each word in the paragraph indicated in parentheses. Use context clues to determine the meaning of the word. Choose the definition that fits the context.

1. proclaimed (3)   a. stated publicly   b. denied privately

2. farcical (5)   a. serious   b. humorous

3. ambiguities (5)   a. uncertainties   b. dangers

4. encroaching (5)   a. getting larger   c. disappearing

5. clandestine (11)   a. sad   b. secret

6. plots (14)   a. plans   b. graves

7. punctured (21)   a. damaged   b. increased

8. epitaph (23)   a. writing on a gravestone   b. fame after one's death

III. Working with Idioms and Expressions

Study the meanings of these idioms and expressions. A form of each one appears in the indicated paragraph of the article.

let it pass (2) refuse to stop or object to something

final resting place (5) a grave

pull someone aside (9) ask someone to talk privately, away from others

give up (12) stop doing or having

mutual fingerpointing (19) blaming one another for causing a problem

make a point (21) make a meaningful statement; make one's opinion clear

Answer these questions.

1. If you are willing to *let an error pass,* do you want it corrected or not?

2. If you engage in *mutual fingerpointing* with a colleague, who is blaming whom?

3. If you *give up* something that you own, what happens to it?

4. If your boss *pulls you aside* and tells you that you have made a mistake, does your boss criticize you in front of other people?

IV. Making Sense of Sentences

Many *appositives* are used in this article. An appositive is a word or phrase placed just after a noun that identifies or renames the noun. Appositives convey important information briefly, without the use of a new sentence.

Example: "just three stones away from Wassermann, <u>Alma's husband</u>" (The underlined words are an appositive. They explain who Wassermann was.)

Match each appositive phrase in column B with the noun that it identifies in column A. For help reread the indicated paragraphs of the article.

A

1. _____ Roger Straus (9)
2. _____ Alma Wassermann (10)
3. _____ Walter Wassermann (10)
4. _____ Janet Hadda (12)
5. _____ Susan Dujack (20)

B

a. a wealthy businessman
b. Alma's granddaughter
c. the author of "Isaac Bashevis Singer: A Life"
d. a founder of Farrar, Straus & Giroux
e. a stylish, self-absorbed German-born refugee

Rewrite the statements by adding information about the person in an appositive phrase. Use the information in the article.

1. <u>Alma Wassermann Singer</u> was not upset about the typo in Singer's tombstone.

   _____

   _____

2. <u>Inge Dujack</u> bought the cemetery plots.

   _____

V. Talking and Writing

Discuss the following topics. Then choose one of them to write about.

1. Does your own family have a family grave site, which is sometimes called a "family plot"? What do you think of this idea? What problems could this idea give rise to?

2. People in some cultures leave flowers on graves to honor the dead. People in other cultures have a "day of the dead," a sort of picnic in the cemetery. What traditions do you have in your own family or culture for honoring the dead?

3. Who is your favorite fiction writer? What kinds of stories does the writer tell? What qualities of the writer appeal to you?

2. Gender Gap at the Movies: Women in the Front Row

Previewing the Article

Do you like "guy movies"? This is a slang term for the sort of Hollywood films that were most successful in the 1980s and the beginning of the 1990s: action-packed, violent movies with little dialogue or character development. The two *Terminator* films with Arnold Schwarzenegger, the *Die Hard* films with Bruce Willis, and the *Lethal Weapon* films with Mel Gibson were very successful with male audiences but not very popular with female ones.

According to this article, female filmgoers are starting to change this situation, for Hollywood producers have discovered that movies that appeal to women can be highly successful as well. The filmmakers are beginning to realize that women demand movies with strong characters, good scripts, and powerful female leads. The most recent example of the power of women audiences at the movies is the astounding success of the film *Titanic*, a romantic story that has proven extremely popular with women.

As this article demonstrates, not only do newspaper readers love movies, but they love the business of the movies as well. This article describes a particular side of the movie industry called *marketing*. Just as athletic shoe companies do surveys and studies to find what kind of shoes consumers would like, so too Hollywood production companies try to discover what kinds of film they should make to earn the greatest possible profits.

Before You Read

Discuss these questions.

1. Do women like different kinds of films from those that men like? What are some examples of films that many women like? What are some examples of films that many men like?

2. Have you ever had a disagreement with a friend of the opposite sex about what movie to see? How did you resolve the problem?

3. What is your favorite film? Why?

As You Read

As you read, look for the answer to this question: Who more often goes alone to movies, men or women?

Gender Gap at Movies: Women in the Front Row

By Bernard Weinraub
New York Times Service

1 LOS ANGELES—After years of making action and adventure films for boys of all ages, studio executives are concluding that a new audience has emerged that is changing all the rules.

2 Women.

3 "Women are now driving the marketplace," said Mark Gill, president of marketing at Miramax. "You ignore this audience at your own peril."

4 William Mechanic, chairman of Fox Filmed Entertainment, said that in an attempt to attract more women to the theaters, female stars are now playing significant, if not dominant, roles in that studio's coming big-budget action films. Among them are "Speed 2: Cruise Control," with Sandra Bullock (and Jason Patric) saving hundreds of passengers on a Caribbean cruise ship threatened by terrorists, and "Alien Resurrection," starring Sigourney Weaver and Winona Ryder, the fourth entry in the "Alien" series.

5 "The aim is to do action films that are more women-friendly, that is, having strong women in top roles and taking out a lot of the violence," Mechanic said. "Women are not only driving the box office but also videocassette rentals and sales and TV watching. Not respecting their taste level is silly."

6 While women have always been important at the box office, studio executives, most of them male, took notice in the last few months when women more or less decided which movies succeeded or failed.

7 "The First Wives Club," the comedy about three women wreaking revenge on husbands who have left them for younger women, was the first and most obvious one. It has grossed $105 million. But women have been central to the success of several disparate films.

8 These include "Jerry Maguire," with Tom Cruise as a sports agent (it was marketed by Tri-Star as a love story, with the sports angle muted); "Michael," in which John Travolta plays an angel who likes women; "Evita," "The English Patient" and "Mother," the Albert Brooks comedy starring Brooks and Debbie Reynolds.

9 "Scream," the Wes Craven horror comedy, can also thank women for the unexpected size of its success. With an overwhelmingly female audience, the modestly

Zade Rosenthal/New Line Cinema

Among films aimed at women: "Michael" with John Travolta as a hell-bent angel.

budgeted movie has taken in nearly $75 million. "It's actually a thriller, not a horror movie," said Gill.

10 It was also women who determined a different fate for several movies aimed directly at them. By largely ignoring "The Evening Star," a sequel to "Terms of Endearment"; "One Fine Day," a comedy about single parents with Michelle Pfeiffer and George Clooney; and "The Preacher's Wife," a fable with Denzel Washington and Whitney Houston—movies that arrived for the Christmas holidays with high expectations—women turned them into major disappointments for their studios.

11 And movie executives said a major reason for the commercial failure of "The People vs. Larry Flynt," which received some of the best reviews of the year, is that women are not going. The movie has been criticized by feminists like Gloria Steinem as glorifying a man whose magazines degrade women. While the film has played well in New York, Los Angeles and other big cities, it has collapsed elsewhere. So far it has grossed almost $19 million.

12 "Women over 25 are very discriminating, very review-sensitive and the toughest to get into the theaters, in contrast to young men," said Sherry Lansing, chairwoman of the Paramount Motion Picture Group. "But when they do come to the theaters, there's a huge audience."

13 Although the last few months have seemed to highlight the strength of women at the box office, some top executives say the trend has been evident for several years. The Motion Picture Association of America, the studio's lobbying arm, said its most recent survey showed that the frequency of women's going to movies had grown somewhat from 1993 to 1995.

14 And while precise figures on attendance by women in the last few months are not available, studio executives say that exit polls at movie houses, telephone surveys and what Gill termed overwhelming anecdotal evidence from theater owners leaves no doubt about the recent impact of women.

15 Laura Ziskin, producer of "Pretty Woman" and "No Way Out," who is now president of Fox 2000, a division of 20th Century Fox that was set up to reach female audiences, said that what had especially surprised her was the influence many women can exert with their husbands or boyfriends in choosing films.

16 Ziskin said that the studio's marketing and research executives had found that while teenage boys tend to make the decisions about what films to see—and girls follow along—just the opposite is true with those in the 30-to-50 category. "If a guy, for example, wants to see 'Showgirls' and the woman doesn't want to, he will see something that she wants to see," Ziskin said.

"They come to a mutual decision."

17 Moreover, she said, the studio has found that men tend to go alone to the movies far more than women, who often go with another woman or in a group.

18 A woman's film can no longer be categorized simply as a comedy or a romance, said Ziskin and others. "A Tom Hanks movie is a woman's film; so is a Tom Cruise or a Harrison Ford movie. 'The Fugitive' was a big woman's movie. So was 'No Way Out.' Women tend to like character-driven movies with strong narrative lines. Movies with sex do appeal to women. Look at 'Fatal Attraction.'"

19 The surge of movies intended to lure female audiences is a result, in part, of the growing number of female studio executives with the power to give the green light to a movie. "You don't say you have to target women, but the reality is, who's making the choices and decisions?" said Stacey Snider, co-president for production at Universal Pictures.

20 Ziskin put it more bluntly: "We've been a testosterone-driven business for a long time. Now I'm looking more at an estrogen-driven business."

21 In traditional Hollywood fashion, the success of "The First Wives Club" has, for the moment, begotten offspring. Bette Midler, one of that film's stars, is now in a comedy, "That Old Feeling," about a divorced couple who start an affair at their daughter's wedding.

22 Another coming comedy, "The Breakers," stars Anjelica Huston and Drew Barrymore as a mother-daughter team of con artists. It is quite likely that "The Breakers" would not have seen the light of day without "The First Wives Club," a number of executives said.

23 "'First Wives Club' convinced us that there's a big audience out there for this kind of picture," said John Davis, producer of "The Breakers."

24 Laurence Mark, a producer of "Jerry Maguire," and of a coming comedy, "Romy and Michelle's High School Reunion," with Lisa Kudrow and Mira Sorvino, said: "When women show up for a movie, they've now proven they can show up in droves and bring their dates in tow. What could be better?"

I. Getting the Message

After reading the article, circle the best answer for each item.

1. *Speed 2: Cruise Control* and *Alien Resurrection* are examples of
   a. romantic films made for female audiences.
   b. films that appeal only to male audiences.
   c. action films with strong female leads.

2. *The First Wives Club* is a film that
   a. was not successful and discouraged studios from making more films about women.
   b. showed studio executives how popular a film about women could be.
   c. was an action film with a strong female lead.

3. One film executive noted that women over 25 tend to
   a. see only romantic films.
   b. go to movies alone.
   c. read film reviews before seeing a movie.

4. Marketing research has shown that
   a. teenage girls make decisions on what films to see on dates.
   b. women from age 30 to 50 tend to go to movies alone or with other women.
   c. men and women from age 30 to 50 make mutual decisions about films to see.

5. One reason that more movies are being made to attract women is that
   a. there are more female movie executives now.
   b. men are becoming less interested in action films.
   c. film executives no longer know how to attract male audiences.

Check your answers with the key on page 117. If you have made mistakes, reread the article to gain a better understanding of it.

II. Expanding Your Vocabulary

A. Getting Meaning from Context

Find each word in the paragraph indicated in parentheses. Use context clues to determine the meaning of the word. Choose the definition that fits the context.

1. dominant (4)   a. main   b. interesting

2. disparate (7)   a. weak   b. different

3. fate (10)   a. outcome   b. start

4. sequel (10)   a. a continuation   b. a display

5. discriminating (12)   a. prejudiced   b. judging quality

6. anecdotal (14)   a. based on personal interviews   b. based on objective tests

7. exert (15)   a. use, have   b. understand, see

8. bluntly (20)   a. disagreeably   b. directly

B. Understanding Adjectives

Two words can be combined with hyphens to create a single adjective. Find each compound adjective in the indicated paragraph. Reread the paragraph. Then circle the letter of the statement that completes the sentence correctly.

1. If a film company has made a *big-budget* (4) action film, it has
   a. made a film about money.
   b. spent a great deal of money making the film.

2. If a film is *women-friendly* (5), it is
   a. about friendly women.
   b. entertaining to women.

3. If a woman is *review-sensitive* (12), she
   a. reads film reviews seriously.
   b. dislikes personal criticism.

4. If a film is *character-driven* (18), it has
   a. very strong characters.
   b. fairly weak characters.

5. If *testosterone-driven* (20) means "led by men," then an *estrogen-driven* (20) film industry makes
   a. many action films with male stars.
   b. many films that appeal to women.

III. Working with Idioms and Expressions

Study the meanings of these idioms and expressions. A form of each one appears in the indicated paragraph of the article.

at your own peril (3) with possibly dangerous results

take in (9) earn

play well (11) be successful

set up (15) create, start

come to a mutual decision (16) agree to do something together

give the green light (19) permit something to be done

beget offspring (21) create similar things

see the light of day (22) be made, come into being

show up in droves (24) come or attend in great numbers

Complete these sentences, using the idioms and expressions.

1. If producers want a movie to _____, they should try to appeal to

   both men and women.

2. Female film executives are more likely to _____ to movies about

   women than male executives.

3. Whether a film stars men or women, movie executives always hope that people will

   _____.

4. When certain kinds of films _____ a lot of money at the box

   office, producers often make more films that are similar.

IV. Analyzing Paragraphs

Skim each group of paragraphs on the left. Then find the statement on the right that indicates the purpose of that group of paragraphs.

1. __e__ Paragraphs 1–5

2. _____ Paragraphs 6–9

3. _____ Paragraphs 10–12

4. _____ Paragraphs 13–18

5. _____ Paragraphs 19–20

6. _____ Paragraphs 21–24

a. give examples of how women's tastes have caused some films to fail

b. give statistics and specific information about women's filmgoing tastes and habits

c. explain how the presence of more female executives has changed the type of films being made

d. indicate which current and future films reflect the new emphasis on women's taste

e. give information about how action films have changed to attract women to see them

f. give examples of films that have succeeded because they attracted women to see them

V. Talking and Writing

Discuss the following topics. Then choose one of them to write about.

1. Do you think Hollywood makes too many action films containing too much violence? Describe some examples.

2. A film *genre* is a kind of film—such as comedies, westerns, science-fiction films, mysteries, police action films, musicals, serious dramas, horror films, romantic films, thrillers. What is your own favorite film *genre* and why?

3. Even though female film stars have been getting more and better roles lately, they still do not make anywhere near the enormous sums of money per film that the top male stars make. Why is this so? Do you think this is fair?

3. Poof! Questions About Magic Go Up in Smoke

Previewing the Article

People love mysteries, and a good magic show presents one mystery after another. This entertaining article is written like a mystery story: the reporter is like a detective who sets out to solve the problem of how magicians do their tricks.

Feature stories are written in different ways. Sometimes the reporter is invisible and simply seems to be the reader's window on a subject. In this kind of objective reporting, there is no *I* in the article, only the third-person *he, she, it,* or *they.* An article written in the first person, however, is more personal, for the writer is a character in the story and organizes it as a narrative.

The reporter-detective in this article investigates the most challenging magician of all, David Copperfield, a performer who has developed the most spectacular tricks of any magician in history. Copperfield was born David Kotkin in New Jersey in 1956 and changed his name to that of a famous character in a novel by Charles Dickens. Whereas other magicians make rabbits disappear, Copperfield has made a seven-ton Lear jet and the Statue of Liberty vanish in front of national television audiences. He has escaped from a steel box on a burning raft sailing toward Niagara Falls; from Alcatraz, the famous prison; from a safe in a building that was destroyed seconds later. His famous show, described in this article, is an astoundingly successful blend of humor, music, special effects, and amazing tricks.

Before You Read

Discuss these questions.

1. Read the headline. The word *poof* describes the puff of smoke that appears just before a magician makes something disappear. *Go up in smoke* is an idiom referring to a sudden disappearance. Rewrite the headline in your own words.

2. Have you ever seen David Copperfield on television? Describe his show. Were you able to guess how he did any of his tricks? If you haven't seen his act, describe any other magic show you have seen.

3. Have you ever tried to do a magic trick yourself? Was it easy or difficult? Tell about your experience.

As You Read

As you read, try to find out whether the reporter was ever satisfied with any of the explanations for how the magic tricks were done.

Poof! Questions About Magic Go Up in Smoke

By Douglas Martin
New York Times Service

Sara Krulwich/The New York Times

1   NEW YORK—Two or three times a day, people fill each of the 1,282 seats of the Martin Beck Theatre. By Sunday, when "Dreams and Nightmares" ends its run, they will have paid more than $6 million to see David Copperfield perform, making his five weeks there the most lucrative in the history of Broadway.

2   My assignment is to find the truth behind the swirling smoke, a path I fear could lead to the essence of magic itself. How does the man who seemed to make the Statue of Liberty disappear do it? Merlin's values, deception and secretiveness, will be tested against a journalist's commitment to literal truth.

3   At least this odd job got me in to the hottest show on Broadway, three times as it turned out. I joined an expectant crowd. "Anybody figured anything out yet?" a man said 20 minutes before the start. A little girl asked her mother if Copperfield would turn her into a rabbit. Maybe.

4   Poof! The star materialized in a suspended elevator. Almost before you could say hocus pocus, a beautiful woman in a red dress was made to evaporate, only to reappear instantly exactly where we thought Copperfield was.

5   Close-up prestidigitations were projected on a screen. People gasped when the magician folded tissue paper into the form of a rose and made it dance a jig. Then he set it afire. Presto! A real crimson rose.

6   All of this coalesced in my mind as a splendiferous blur, the precise intention. It happened the next day, too. But as for the question that percolated through the entranced crowd like a mantra—"How did he do that?"—I was clueless.

7   Experts might tell. I made my way to Flosso-Hornmann Magic Co., near Herald Square, founded in 1856 and once owned by Harry Houdini. The current owner, Jacki Flosso, a magician himself, delivered the dismissive message I would hear repeatedly: Those who know do not speak, and those who speak do not know.

8   At another emporium, Magic Max in Times Square, the reply was the same. "I could tell you how he does it," said John Feliciano, the counter man. "But it's not right."

9   Things were no less frustrating when I visited Joseph Gabriel, a nimble magician performing off Broadway at the Lamb's Theatre. His finale involves making a New York cab instantly materialize, the ultimate New York miracle.

10   So just how does he think Copperfield does levitations? "Very well," replied Gabriel, smirking.

11   Next was David Roth, called "the best coin man in the world." He likened the exposure of magical technique to a documentary on the making of "Star Wars" that showed the starship Galactica as a small model. Seeing this, he said, made it impossible to be awed by the vehicle. "You can never again see the magic," he said.

12   This profession of tricksters was beginning to seem the tightest of fraternities. Its clubhouse is the coffee shop of the Edison Hotel on West 47th Street in Manhattan, where magicians have hung out for more than half a century.

13   Mike Bronstein, introduced as "host of the magicians' table," said it was better not to know how wonders happened for the same reason

that undressing an attractive woman can diminish her allure. But Jim McGrath, a confederate, volunteered to tell all.

14   "The secret is Abracadabra, the magic word," he said solemnly. "Some magicians might use another word, of course."

15   Thanks. And the competition, The New York Post, had just scooped me with a splashy article saying Copperfield's illusions were facilitated by salting the crowd with paid "stooges" to pose as volunteers. This was something I had begun to suspect. But I urgently needed help and begged a magically inclined friend to attend the show with me.

16   As the show began, she said, "The fact the background is black and the lights are pointing out at you means he can get away with murder. Whatever he was going to do, he's already done it."

17   Her theories flowed like a welcome river. Is it possible those are someone else's toes on the lower half of the magician? Could Copperfield have a double? Is it possible the woman in the red dress has an onstage twin? The light silhouetting Copperfield's form almost surely alters the perception of where he really is, she whispered.

18   When Copperfield reappeared for the second act in a bulky sweater, she immediately suspected he was concealing harnesses for his flight. But wait a minute. Weren't hoops passed over Copperfield's airborne body? Her response: Magician's hoops are always rigged.

19   All this amounts only to very informed suspicion. I next clicked on one of the many magicians' chat rooms on the World Wide Web. One message says that Copperfield uses audience plants in "a host of his effects." Another calls his flying "beautiful, if boring" and gives the name of the rigging company the message writer is convinced made his harness.

20   At this point, lightning struck, an investigative reporter's dream: a disgruntled employee. An anonymous caller said he worked as an audience plant in the show, specifically one of the seeming volunteers who rise high above the stage on a levitating couch. He was angry about repeatedly being paid his $40 a performance late.

21   I said I could not trust him unless he gave me his name. He said he would think about it. He called back and gave it to me: Seth Greenspan. To prove his validity, he produced 11 used complimentary tickets he had picked up at the box office so he would appear to be just another paying customer.

22   Greenspan told a tale of immensely sophisticated legerdemain. But was it reasonable to believe that the 20 or so audience plants assembled an hour before shows in Room 1055 of the Ramada Inn, as he said? His tale of watching Copperfield coach identical twins seemed like science fiction.

23   If true, what should be made of this? The person to ask was Charles Reynolds, one of the great inventors of magical tricks. He orchestrated Doug Henning's and Harry Blackstone Jr.'s Broadway

shows, devising different ways for each to make an elephant disappear.

24 "Look, you can't write this story," he said. "You'll hurt David, and, more important, you'll hurt magic."

25 Reynolds explained that all of magic consisted of perhaps a dozen tricks—appearing to cut a person in half, walking through walls and so on—with myriad variations. What is important, he said, is the overall theatrical effect. Nobody questions whether Hamlet's sword really drips blood.

26 What magicians do, Reynolds said, is by definition harmless, completely different from the deception of a three-card monte artist, though the sleight of hand is similar. Magicians don't deceive; they control the perception of willing people.

27 "Everybody wants to believe in magic," he said. "If you tell how illusions work, it's like telling children there is no Santa Claus."

I. Getting the Message

After reading the article, circle the best answer for each item.

1. David Copperfield's Broadway show is
   a. a disappointment to the reporter.
   b. extremely popular.
   c. moderately successful.

2. An article in another newspaper claimed that Copperfield
   a. paid people to pretend to be audience members and help him do tricks.
   b. was not an experienced magician.
   c. used video cameras to perform his tricks.

3. The reporter's friend pointed out
   a. her theories of how some tricks were done.
   b. exactly how Copperfield performed all the tricks.
   c. why it is impossible ever to know how magicians perform their tricks.

4. Charles Reynolds, the inventor of magic tricks, believes that
   a. all magicians should explain how they do their tricks.
   b. explaining magic is not really possible.
   c. explaining magic destroys all the fun of it.

5. In his research the reporter discovered
   a. exactly how Copperfield does most of his tricks.
   b. how to do tricks himself.
   c. that magicians do not like to reveal their methods.

Check your answers with the key on page 117. If you have made mistakes, reread the article to gain a better understanding of it.

II. Expanding Your Vocabulary

Getting Meaning from Context

Find each word in the paragraph indicated in parentheses. Use context clues to determine the meaning of the word. Choose the definition that fits the context.

1. run (1) a. a race b. a series of performances

2. lucrative (1) a. moneymaking b. entertaining

3. deception (2) a. trickery b. revelation

4. coalesced (6) a. came together b. became cold

5. splendiferous (6) a. painful b. wonderful

6. emporium (8) a. a large store b. a palace

7. scooped (15) a. printed the story first b. attacked as unimportant

8. splashy (15) a. wet b. showy

9. pose (15) a. cause a problem b. act as someone else to deceive

10. disgruntled (20) a. unhappy b. uneducated

III. Working with Idioms and Expressions

Answer these questions with **yes** or **no.** Pay particular attention to the meanings of the expressions in bold print. Each expression appears in the indicated paragraph of the article. Explain your answers.

1. If you **figure something out** (3), do you know the answer? _____

2. If you **are clueless** (6) about a problem, do you understand it? _____

3. When people **hang out** (12) somewhere, do they go there often? _____

4. If a magician **gets away with murder** (16) in regard to a trick, is the trick successful?

   _____

5. If **lightning strikes** (20) a reporter looking for information, is the reporter injured?

   _____

IV. Analyzing Paragraphs

The paragraphs in this article are arranged chronologically, like a detective story. The writer, who is the main character, or protagonist, of the story, is presented with a mystery and then goes to various locations and talks to people who can help him solve the mystery.

Circle the best answer to each item.

1. Paragraphs 1–2 introduce the article by
   a. presenting the problem the writer is tying to solve.
   b. presenting the problem and some possible solutions.
   c. giving the biography of David Copperfield.

2. Paragraphs 3–6 develop the narrative or story by describing
   a. the history of magic.
   b. a magic performance.
   c. David Copperfield's theory of magic.

3. Paragraphs 7–14 further develop the story by reporting
   a. interviews with experts.
   b. public attitudes toward magic.
   c. trends in the performance of magic.

4. Paragraphs 15–18 show the writer's attempts to find answers by
   a. attempting to learn magic himself.
   b. interviewing teachers of magic at universities.
   c. attending another David Copperfield performance with a friend.

5. Paragraph 19 reports the author's attempts to find answers from
   a. the Internet.
   b. research in the magic section of a large library.
   c. a historian of magic.

6. Paragraphs 20–22 present the explanations of
   a. a world-famous expert.
   b. someone who claimed to be an ex-employee of the show.
   c. the owner of a magic shop.

7. Paragraphs 23–27 present the climax of the story—the final solution to the mystery posed at the beginning—in the form of an interview
   a. with the manager of the theater where Copperfield performs.
   b. with David Copperfield himself.
   c. presenting the views of an inventor of magic tricks.

V. Talking and Writing

Discuss the following topics. Then choose one of them to write about.

1. Do you like or dislike magic shows and acts? Why?

2. Do you think that professional magicians should reveal how the tricks are done? Why or why not? Would you like to know how the tricks are done? Do you have any ideas to explain the tricks?

3. Reread paragraph 24. Do you agree that Copperfield's act and other magic are harmless even though they involve deception? What are the reasons for your opinion?

4. What mystery really interests you? It may be a mystery in history, such as why monuments of early peoples were built. It may be a mystery in nature—for example, how animals, such as whales and dolphins, communicate. What ideas, or theories, have been proposed to explain the mystery? Do you think there will ever be a clear answer to the mystery?

Focus on the Newspaper

The newspaper provides information about events in the world of arts and entertainment. It is a handy, up-to-date, inexpensive source of information about ways to spend leisure time.

Objective Articles

Some articles about cultural events and entertainment are objective accounts, providing just the facts. This type of story tells when a particular concert, movie, play, or art exhibit will (or did) open, how long it will be in town, and how much it costs. The story also describes the content, identifies the artists, and discusses the size and scope of the show. This sort of article is likely to appear in the paper shortly before or immediately after a particular cultural event opens. At the same time, you can expect to see advertisements for the event in the paper.

Exercise 1: Comparing an Arts or Entertainment News Story and an Ad

Cut out a newspaper article about a live performance, art exhibit, or movie that has just opened or is about to open in your city. Look for an article that is not a review (an evaluation) but simply tells about the show. Then find an advertisement for the same event. Answer these questions about the article and the ad.

1. Compare the article and the ad. What are the main differences in purpose?

2. What are the main differences in content?

3. After reading the ad, did you want to see this show or exhibit? Why or why not?

4. After reading the article, did you want to see it? Why or why not?

Reviews

Newspapers often give readers opinions on various forms of entertainment. They answer readers' questions: Should I see this play or movie, buy this book, or visit this museum? Is it worth my time and money? Will I enjoy it or learn from it? A good review does several things. It describes, analyzes, and evaluates. If informs readers about how a particular work compares to others of the same type. It also gives readers an opinion about the strengths, weaknesses, and overall quality of a work.

Exercise 2: Comparing an Objective Article and a Review

Scan the newspaper for a review of the event described in your article for exercise 1. (There will probably be one within a week or so.) What is the reviewer's overall recommendation? Does the reviewer suggest going to see this event or not? Does the reviewer's judgment surprise you? Tell why or why not.

Exercise 3: Comparing a Reviewer's Opinion with Your Own

Find a newspaper review of a movie or TV show you saw, a concert you attended, or a book you read. List four of the reviewer's evaluative points and tell whether you agree or disagree with each one. Overall, did the reviewer like the event or book? Did you?

Exercise 4: Reviewing the Reviews

Look in the entertainment section of a newspaper. Select three reviews to read: they may be of movies, plays, concerts, art exhibits, or other artistic works or forms of entertainment. (Note: Some newspapers have a daily entertainment section that contains reviews. Others have a special weekly section with reviews of current entertainment or books.) Read the reviews carefully. Then complete a chart like this.

Analyzing a Review

Type of Entertainment (Movie, Concert, etc.)	Name of Entertainment	Brief Description	Strengths	Weaknesses	Reviewer's Overall Evaluation

Exercise 5: You Be the Reviewer

Prepare a short review of some leisure-time activity you have enjoyed (or not enjoyed) recently. Tell whether or not you recommend this particular activity and why.

SCIENCE/ HEALTH

Focus on the Newspaper: Science / Health

1. Picky Eater: New Image for the Great White Shark

Previewing the Article

Have you ever gone swimming in the ocean and worried that you could become a tasty lunch for a shark? According to recent research, you may have too high an opinion of yourself. As this fascinating article suggests, new studies into the eating habits of sharks show that humans are not an attractive menu item for these fierce fish.

The reason for the public's misunderstanding is obvious: sharks look scary. The 1975 hit film *Jaws* contributed to this image of the shark as a frightening creature. This movie's shark was enormous and showed a special interest in people: it regularly visited a particular beach, as it would a favorite restaurant. However, our fear of sharks and other animals, such as snakes and wolves, may go beyond the actual dangers such animals pose.

The article examines the great white shark, the kind most people think of when they imagine dangerous sharks. In fact, there are as many as 370 species of shark, ranging in size from the whale shark, which can measure 49 feet and is the largest fish in the sea, to the smallest kind, which is only 6 to 8 inches in length. And some are surprisingly nondangerous— the enormous whale shark eats mainly plankton, the tiny animal and plant life floating on the ocean surface.

This article shows the valuable role newspapers can play in educating the public about nature and science and in contradicting some very commonly held mistaken ideas.

Before You Read

Discuss these questions.

1. What do you know about sharks? Have you ever seen them in the ocean or in an aquarium? Describe the ones you have seen.

2. Have you seen the film *Jaws* or any of the three later *Jaws* films? How are sharks portrayed in these movies? Did the films influence your idea of sharks?

3. What are the most terrifying animals to you? Why are they so terrifying?

As You Read

As you read, find out what normally happens when a shark attacks a human being.

Picky Eater: New Image for the Great White Shark

By William J. Broad
New York Times Service

1   NEW YORK—Few animals have the power to frighten people into the cold terror of being eaten alive. But the great white shark does so effortlessly. Its reputation for blood lust is rooted in images of jaws gleaming with rows of razor-sharp teeth, their edges nicely serrated to ease the job of tearing through bone and flesh.

2   Nature's great killing machine grows to lengths of 20 feet (6 meters) or more and is often viewed as crude and mindlessly malevolent, feeding just as heartily on humans as on fish, seals, whales and sea lions. But new research is challenging that notion and shedding light on the hidden life of the great white, revealing a finicky eater that may find people unpalatable.

3   Though it is pitiless with prey, lunging and slashing in red-stained water, the species can be quite civil among its own. Scientists have found what appears to be a ritualized competition over kills in which two great whites will forgo attacking one another for a genteel bout of slapping tails on the sea's surface. The biggest splash decides the winner. Such finesse stands in stark contrast to the raw violence among predators like wolves, which can engage one another in bloody fights to the death.

4   Over all, scientists say, great whites have been badly misunderstood, wrongly making them the demons of movies and nightmares. Some research has even found evidence that the killers, when thwarted in feeding, get visibly frustrated and agitated, perhaps even sad and dejected.

5   "We're dispelling myths and learning a lot about how they really live," said Dr. A. Peter Klimley, a biologist at the University of California Bodega Marine Laboratory in Bodega Bay, California, who is a prominent expert on the infamous shark. "They're not stupid feeding machines. They're exquisitely adapted."

6   Dr. Douglas J. Long, a fish scientist at the California Academy of Sciences who studies great whites, said the new insights, while substantial, still left a greater number of riddles. "For instance," Dr. Long said, "we know virtually nothing about how and where they mate."

7   Even as scientists seek to unravel the great white's biology, behavior and ecology, a political push is accelerating to protect the beast. The top predator of the sea, it

Source: "Great White Sharks," A. P. Klimley and D. G. Ainley (Academic Press)

Ritual Combat Over Dinner

After a kill by two male sharks, scientists observed them in a splashing display to determine who got the carcass, first swimming past each other without touching, then rolling over slightly to splash water in the other's direction. The shark that managed to stir up the most water in several passes got the meal.

appears to be declining in numbers because of assaults by sport fishermen as well as commercial interests serving a growing international market for white-shark jaws and teeth. California, South Africa and Australia have taken steps to try to save the great white, and other states and countries are considering such conservation efforts.

8   Its numbers "will inevitably dwindle unless prudent controls are enacted," Dr. Richard C. Murphy, a marine ecologist at the Cousteau Society in Chesapeake, Virginia, wrote in "Great White Sharks," a collection of scientific reports published late last year by Academic Press.

9   "In addition to being increasingly rare," Dr. Murphy said, "they are majestic preeminent participants in a complicated food web which we, as yet, only partially understand."

10   Sharks are ancient animals, long predating the dinosaurs. Carcharodon carcharias, or "ragged tooth" in scholarly Latin, is found in temperate waters throughout the world's seas. To find prey, it has sensors known as lateral-line organs that apparently can detect disturbances in sea water at ranges of a mile or more.

11   Closer to a victim (exactly how close is uncertain), its keen ears can hear thrashing, its sensitive nose can sniff blood, and its

eerie black eyes can spy flesh. Powerful muscles send it lunging.

12   The triangular teeth grow to lengths of two or more inches and are extraordinarily strong. Three layers of enamel crisscross in different directions so the teeth can better withstand impact as well as twisting and bending. If a tooth is lost, a replacement directly behind it will rotate forward in a day or so. New teeth are constantly being formed in this replacement process.

13   Judging from stomach contents, the beast can indeed devour prey whole, including other sharks and sea lions. Though one of its nicknames is "man-eater" (another is "white death"), no one knows for certain if people are in fact a preferred food.

14   To explore such questions, scientists in the last decade have increasingly studied the beast's predatory habits. Dr. Klimley of the Bodega Marine Laboratory, working with Peter Pyle and Scot D. Anderson, did a pioneering study near the Farallon Islands, which lie some 30 miles west of San Francisco in one of the most productive fisheries on the West Coast. Video recordings were made of 129 great-white attacks on seals and sea lions, the assaults rich in explosive splashes in bloodstained water.

15 An analysis suggested that a shark near the surface would bite its victim, drag it down bleeding, carry it underwater and perhaps take another bite, then let the carcass float upward. If the victim was still alive, the act might be repeated. The shark's aim, the scientists deduced, was to have the prey bleed to death as soon as possible, minimizing a violent struggle.

16 In an interview, Dr. Klimley noted that attacks on people often followed a similar pattern—but the sharks, after dragging humans down, bleeding, often let them go.

17 Dr. Klimley said white sharks might spit out humans, birds and sea otters because their bodies lacked the energy-rich layers of fat possessed by seals and whales. "If they ingest something that's not energetically profitable, then they're stuck with that for a few days" of slow digestion, he said. "Fat has twice the energy value of muscle."

I. Getting the Message

After reading the article, circle the best answer for each item.

1. When people think fearfully of sharks, they imagine
   a. how fast sharks can swim.
   b. the trouble they cause for large ships.
   c. rows of very sharp teeth.

2. When sharks eat their prey, they
   a. can be surprisingly nonviolent with each other.
   b. are always extremely violent with each other.
   c. compete violently the way wolves do.

3. Scientists do not understand very much about
   a. how sharks eat.
   b. how sharks mate.
   c. what sharks like to hunt.

4. Sharks can detect prey
   a. a mile away.
   b. only a few feet away.
   c. by communicating with other sharks.

5. Great white sharks are hunted by fishing companies for their
   a. tails and fins.
   b. jaws and teeth.
   c. eggs.

6. Current research shows that sharks are disappointed when they bite into a human because
   a. they prefer fattier food.
   b. humans have too many bones.
   c. humans struggle too much.

Check your answers with the key on page 117. If you have made mistakes, reread the article to gain a better understanding of it.

II. Expanding Your Vocabulary

A. Getting Meaning from Context

Find each word in the paragraph indicated in parentheses. Use context clues to determine the meaning of the word. Choose the definition that fits the context.

1. effortlessly (1)	a. happily	b. easily
2. serrated (1)	a. jagged, like a saw	b. sharp
3. forgo (3)	a. give up	b. begin
4. finesse (3)	a. skill	b. violence
5. thwarted (4)	a. helped	b. blocked, stopped
6. dispelling (5)	a. making simple	b. showing not to be true
7. riddles (6)	a. puzzle answers	b. unexplained items
8. temperate (10)	a. calm, not moving	b. warm
9. extraordinarily (12)	a. beyond the ordinary	b. very ordinary

B. Understanding Adjectives

Match each adjective in column A with its definition in column B. Look for the adjective in the paragraph indicated in parentheses.

A	B
1. _____ crude (2)	a. sensible
2. _____ malevolent (2)	b. not good to eat
3. _____ unpalatable (2)	c. polite
4. _____ civil (3)	d. large in number
5. _____ dejected (4)	e. strange and causing fear
6. _____ substantial (6)	f. very sad and depressed
7. _____ prudent (8)	g. violent and noisy
8. _____ eerie (11)	h. without manners or feeling
9. _____ predatory (14)	i. evil, bad
10. _____ explosive (14)	j. hunting

C. Practicing Useful Vocabulary

Complete the sentences below with words from column A in exercise B, above.

1. Scientists are learning more about the _____ habits of sharks. They

   now know more about how sharks kill their victims.

2. There are still _____ questions about how sharks behave in nature.

   Scientists have a lot more to learn.

3. The idea that a powerful and violent great white shark would feel

   _____ when having trouble eating sounds rather funny.

4. Scientists have learned that sharks sometimes attack people, but they let them go. They

   think that sharks find people _____.

III. Working with Idioms and Expressions

Find each italicized phrase in the indicated paragraph of the article. Circle the answer that conveys the meaning of the phrase correctly.

1. The great white shark has a *reputation for blood lust* (1). This means that the shark
   a. is thought to enjoy killing.
   b. has been known as a fish that bleeds.

2. Research is *shedding light on the hidden life* (2) of the great white shark. It is
   a. explaining things about the shark not known previously.
   b. using bright lights to show where sharks are hiding.

3. The great white shark is a *finicky eater* (2) and not a crude, hearty eater. This means it
   a. eats and chews slowly and carefully.
   b. likes to eat certain things better than others.

4. The splashing ritual of the shark *stands in stark contrast to the raw violence* (3) of wolves. This means that the shark is
   a. as violent as a wolf.
   b. less violent than a wolf.

5. If some countries *have taken steps to save the great white* (7), they have
    a. already saved the shark.
    b. begun to try to save the shark.

6. If a shark is *stuck with* (17) a hard-to-digest meal, it
    a. must take a few days to digest the meal.
    b. enjoys its meal but has to eat slowly.

IV. Analyzing Paragraphs

Paragraphs usually have one main or key idea. Match each of these main ideas with one of these paragraphs: 4, 7, 12, 14, and 17.

Main Idea   **Paragraph Number**

1. Great white sharks need food that is rich in fat, so humans are not good prey for sharks.   _____

2. Scientists have studied the great white shark's feeding habits with video cameras.   _____

3. Because the number of great white sharks is going down, some governments are trying to save them.   _____

4. Great white sharks are not the monsters people usually think they are.   _____

5. The great white shark's teeth are perfectly suited for the job of attacking and eating prey and can quickly be replaced.   _____

V. Talking and Writing

Discuss the following topics. Then choose one of them to write about.

1. This article is about a misconception—that is, a mistaken idea—that people have about a well-known animal. Can you think of any other misconceptions that people have about animals? What kinds of animals seem particularly misunderstood?

2. This article maintains that sharks are not as dangerous to humans as most people think. Do you think this fact should change the way swimmers feel about the dangers of sharks? What other dangers should ocean swimmers be on the alert for?

3. What animal are you most afraid of? Why? Is there an animal that you do not fear but others do? What is it?

4. Do you think that people should spend time and money to study animal behavior? Why or why not?

2. Evaluating Acupuncture: Medical Profession Is Divided

Would you consider having a doctor stick needles in various parts of your body to relieve the pain of a headache? If so, you are among the growing number of people who are turning to the ancient Eastern practice of acupuncture as a method of pain relief.

Before the early 1970s, however, most people in the United States would have thought this solution to pain was simply crazy. The big change in attitude was partly brought about by the respected *New York Times* columnist James Reston. While in China reporting on President Richard Nixon's visit to that country in July of 1971, Reston had an emergency operation to remove his appendix. To relieve Reston's intense pain after the operation, a doctor inserted long needles into his knees and elbow, and the pain disappeared. Reston's articles about this experience helped acupuncture gain acceptance in the United States.

As this informative article shows, the medical profession in the United States has begun to accept acupuncture as a pain-relief procedure, but it still is uncertain about many aspects of it. One problem is that acupuncture is based on an ancient Chinese idea of the body that modern Western science does not accept. The idea is that the body has vital energy that travels along pathways. When the vital energy is misdirected in illness, the acupuncture needles push it back along the proper pathway.

Another problem is that acupuncturists are holistic—that is, they see the emotions and the body as closely connected. In contrast, modern Western medicine tends to treat a patient's various medical problems as isolated, separate issues.

Before You Read

Discuss these questions.

1. What do you know about acupuncture? Have you or has anyone you know ever had this treatment? Was the treatment effective?

2. What is meant by the term "alternative medicine"? How does it differ from the standard medicine of the American Medical Association?

3. Does your doctor take the time to give you "TLC," that is, the "tender loving care" of talking to you about your daily habits on a typical visit? Should a doctor do this?

As You Read

As you read, find the immediate occasion—the news-related reason—for this report about the benefits of acupuncture.

Evaluating Acupuncture: Medical Profession Is Divided

By Jane E. Brody
New York Times Service

1 NEW YORK—In 1971, James Reston, The New York Times columnist, underwent an emergency appendectomy in China and described acupuncture's success in relieving his postoperative pain.

2 Since then, acupuncture has flourished in the West, mainly among lay practitioners trained in this technique, in which certain points are stimulated on or under the skin, mostly with ultrafine needles.

3 Although acupuncture does not cure anything, advocates of the technique say that for many common health problems, especially those involving chronic pain, acupuncture is at least as effective as standard medical remedies like drugs and surgery and usually safer.

4 Still, mainstream medicine has been reluctant to endorse acupuncture as a potentially valuable tool, citing as its main reasons scientifically inadequate studies, mystical explanations of how the technique works, the risk of misdiagnoses and the possibility of hazards from medically unsupervised treatments.

5 Patients, meanwhile, have been voting with their pocketbooks. In 1993, the Food and Drug Administration reported that more than a million Americans spent about $500 million each year to get up to 12 million acupuncture treatments. Patients pay for most of those treatments because few insurers cover them.

6 Are these patients simply buying an expensive placebo, or do therapeutic benefits emerge from acupuncture treatments?

7 This month, experts who were asked by the consensus development program of the National Institutes of Health to summarize the best available tests of acupuncture's effects found several well-documented benefits and the potential for many more for which rigorous scientific proof is not available.

8 Patients most often seek acupuncture to relieve painful conditions that fail to go away on their own, that do not respond well to standard treatments or that may require more hazardous remedies, like surgery or the long-term use of potent drugs. An independent panel evaluating the reports concluded that acupuncture could alleviate acute pain—for example, postoperative pain—and might also help control chronic pain, like chronic migraines, neck pain, muscle pain and osteoarthritis of the knee. The panel also found acupuncture to be highly effective in combating nausea caused by pregnancy, anesthesia or cancer chemotherapy.

9 Presentations to the consensus conference made it all too clear why the American medical establishment has failed to give acupuncture its blessing. Without big money to underwrite large long-term studies of acupuncture's potential contribution to healing, the overwhelming majority of studies have involved too few patients and too little time to prove anything one way or another.

10 Researchers debated how best to study acupuncture. Should it be compared with no treatment, an inactive placebo or sham acupuncture (which in itself has some effects), or should it be mea-

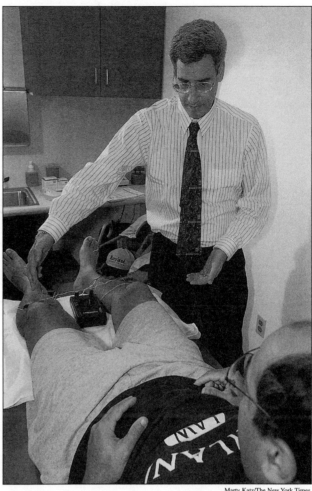

Marty Katz/The New York Times

Dr. Brian Berman treating a patient in Maryland for knee pain.

sured against standard medical therapies? Should the results be assessed by someone other than the acupuncturist? Should patients who previously had acupuncture be excluded from the studies? Or should only those patients who are known to respond positively to acupuncture be studied? And to determine whether acupuncture is effective, which of the more than 2,000 points on the human body should be needled, how often and for how long?

11 Dr. Steve Birch of the APT Foundation in New Haven, Connecticut, said that an adequate test of acupuncture for chronic pain should involve needling at 10 sites for at least 10 treatments. "But none of the headache studies I reviewed met these criteria," he reported. At best, Dr. Birch could say that acupuncture was better than an inactive placebo and roughly equivalent to standard headache therapy. But since the treatment of chronic headaches involves medications that often have unpleasant side effects, acupuncture may be preferable because it rarely causes side effects.

12 Another consideration is the therapeutic milieu. Practitioners of traditional Chinese medicine challenged the design of acupuncture studies that ignore its usual holistic therapeutic context, which often involves "TLC," herbal remedies and individualized treatment based on each patient's unique characteristics. In other words, it may not be possible to strip the art from the science of acupuncture and end up with a meaningful result.

13 Another question is whether the observed benefits of acupuncture can be explained physiologically. Researchers at the consensus conference cited several biological effects of acupuncture that might account for its benefits. These include the release in the brain

and spinal cord of chemicals that subdue pain and transmit messages to nerves and muscles, as well as hormonal changes and increases in cerebral blood flow and immune function.

14 Rather than viewing acupuncture as an "alternative" treatment, patients should regard it as complementary to standard medical practice, researchers and many practitioners at the meeting said.

15 Before seeking treatments from an acupuncturist, patients should see a doctor to determine the diagnosis and weigh the standard therapeutic options. As one practitioner noted, treating pain of unknown origin with acupuncture can mask a serious underlying condition and delay the correct diagnosis and treatment, sometimes with serious, even fatal, consequences.

16 And note: Insist that any acupuncturist use sterile, disposable needles. This will avoid the most frequent risk of acupuncture—transmission of an infectious disease like hepatitis or AIDS.

I. Getting the Message

After reading the article, indicate whether each statement is true (**T**) or false (**F**).

1. _____ The main purpose of this article is to report what the current attitude of the medical profession in the United States is toward acupuncture.

2. _____ Acupuncture has been shown to cure many diseases.

3. _____ One of the most common reasons for using acupuncture is to relieve long-lasting pain that won't go away.

4. _____ Researchers do not agree about the best way to determine the effectiveness of acupuncture.

5. _____ Scientists now completely understand how acupuncture works on the body.

6. _____ Studies show that acupuncture causes many unpleasant side effects.

7. _____ The article is basically positive about the benefits of acupuncture but cautions the reader about using it.

Check your answers with the key on page 117. If you have made mistakes, reread the article to gain a better understanding of it.

II. Expanding Your Vocabulary

A. Getting Meaning from Context

Find each word in the paragraph indicated in parentheses. Use context clues to determine the meaning of the word. Choose the definition that fits the context.

1. flourished (2)	a. been successful	b. been unknown
2. practitioners (2)	a. those learning a subject	b. those using their subject knowledge
3. chronic (3)	a. for a limited time	b. constant, not going away

4. endorse (4)   a. approve   b. examine

5. potentially (4)   a. obviously   b. possibly

6. alleviate (8)   a. help   b. make worse

7. underwrite (9)   a. compose, write   b. provide money for

8. complementary (14)   a. finishing, going together with   b. opposed to, working against

B. Studying Vocabulary About Medicine

Find each term from column A in the indicated paragraph of the article. Reread the paragraph. Then match each term with its definition in column B.

A

1. _____ appendectomy (1)

2. _____ postoperative pain (1)

3. _____ placebo (6)

4. _____ anesthesia (8)

5. _____ side effects (11)

6. _____ therapeutic milieu (12)

7. _____ cerebral blood flow (13)

8. _____ immune function (13)

B

a. treatment to keep a surgical patient from feeling pain

b. the body's disease-fighting system

c. environment in which a treatment occurs

d. operation to remove the appendix

e. pain after an operation

f. an unexpected result on the body

g. pill or treatment with no real healing power

h. the circulation of blood in the brain

III. Working with Idioms and Expressions

Find each italicized expression in the indicated paragraph of the article. Reread the paragraph. Then answer the question.

1. Are the doctors in the American *medical establishment* (9) considered to be in *mainstream medicine* (4) or *alternative treatment* (14)?

2. If people are *voting with their pocketbooks* (5) for acupuncture, are they spending money or not spending money on acupuncture?

3. If American doctors have failed to *give* acupuncture their *blessing* (9), have they not studied acupuncture or have they not agreed that acupuncture is a good thing to use?

4. If studies can't *prove anything one way or another* (9), are they successful?

5. If a person is *weighing options* (15), has the person made a decision yet?

This article has an objective tone because it reports the findings of a consensus of doctors in the United States about the value of acupuncture. As such, the article simply reports the positive and negative aspects of acupuncture as these doctors see them.

In this exercise decide whether the statement taken from the article is positive about the value of acupuncture (**P**) or negative about its value (**N**).

1. Advocates believe that acupuncture is at least as effective as standard medical remedies. (3) _____

2. Mainstream medicine has been reluctant to endorse acupuncture as a potentially valuable tool. (4) _____

3. Americans spent about $500 million each year to get up to 12 million acupuncture treatments. (5) _____

4. A report concluded that acupuncture could alleviate acute pain. (8) _____

5. Since the treatment of chronic headaches involves medications that often have unpleasant side effects, acupuncture may be preferable because it rarely causes side effects. (11) _____

6. Treating pain of unknown origin with acupuncture can mask a serious underlying condition and delay the correct diagnosis and treatment. (15) _____

V. Talking and Writing

Discuss the following topics. Then choose one of them to write about.

1. After reading this article, do you think you would try acupuncture for serious pain? Why or why not? What are some of its dangers? What are some of its positive aspects?

2. What are some of the reasons that many people have become dissatisfied with conventional medicine? Is their dissatisfaction justified?

3. These are some forms of alternative medicine popular today: chiropractic, naprapathy, exercise therapy, herbalism, and homeopathy. What do you know about them?

4. What did you learn about the scientific method as applied to medical treatment from this article? What are some ways scientists have tried to show the effects of acupuncture?

Focus on the Newspaper

Newspapers print articles on scientific topics when the information is of interest or importance to the general public. The discovery of a new chemical element, research leading to new insights about disease, analyses of the causes of an earthquake—all these matters of "hard" science need to be explained to the general reading public in understandable, nontechnical ways.

The social sciences are also frequent topics of articles. Social sciences deal primarily with people and how they live now or lived in the past. Fields such as psychology, sociology, and anthropology examine how people function individually and in groups. Archaeologists study past cultures and often dig up artifacts revealing much about the lives of ancient peoples. Science articles in newspapers cover a variety of topics.

Explanations in Science Articles

Journalists must be careful to make technical material meaningful to readers who are not specialists in the field. Science-related articles often include definitions, examples, comparisons, reasons, and statistics (numerical facts) to help readers understand scientific findings.

Exercise 1: Dissecting a Science Article

Find an article about a science or social science topic in the newspaper. Number the paragraphs in the article. Then read it, looking for the information to complete the chart.

Analyzing a Science Article

Did you find . . .	Yes	No	Paragraph Number(s)
1. a definition?	_____	_____	_____
2. an example?	_____	_____	_____
3. a comparison?	_____	_____	_____
4. a statistic?	_____	_____	_____
5. a problem?	_____	_____	_____
6. a solution?	_____	_____	_____
7. a discovery?	_____	_____	_____
8. a recommendation?	_____	_____	_____
9. contrasting points of view?	_____	_____	_____

Articles on Ecology

Ecology is the branch of science that deals with the relationship between living things and their environment. In recent years, there has been a lot of public concern about the environment throughout the world. Newspapers frequently print articles about air, water, and land pollution and about damage to plants and animals. These articles can be divided into two main categories: (1) those that tell about present or future harm; and (2) those that tell about efforts to improve the environment.

Exercise 2: Articles About the Environment

Find a newspaper article on some aspect of ecology. Then answer these questions about it.

1. What is the main idea of this article? State it in one sentence.

2. Who or what is affected by the subject of the article?

3. Does this article make you feel optimistic or pessimistic about the environment on Earth in the future?

4. What is the source of the information in the article?

5. Do you think this is an objective source, or does this person, group, business, or industry have a bias? Would the person or group benefit from making things sound better or worse than they really are?

Articles on Health Care

Newspapers often print news stories about the latest in medical research and treatment. Many papers also print regular columns by physicians and other health-care experts. In these columns the experts answer questions from readers and give advice about physical and mental health.

Daily newspapers are an important source of information about advances in the field of medicine. Newspapers perform a great service by telling people how to take better care of themselves.

Exercise 3: It's Your Health

Scan the headlines of three newspapers to find articles and columns about health care. Select two articles or columns to read and analyze. Write this information about each article:

1. What is the most important scientific fact stated in the article?

2. Did you know this fact before reading it here?

3. Is there a stated or implied recommendation about changing behavior to become healthier (for example, avoid smoking or eating fats)?

SPORTS

1. In Nagano, Cross-Cultural Tensions

Previewing the Article

At the end of the opening ceremonies of the 1998 winter Olympics in Nagano, Japan, television audiences all over the world were treated to a spectacular show of international harmony and goodwill. Giant choruses on five continents sang Beethoven's inspiring "Ode to Joy." The cooperation and organization evident in such a beautiful performance was even more amazing in the light of the cultural tensions that accompanied the Olympic games, which in 1998 involved athletes from a record 72 nations.

This article explains the nature of some of those tensions, which ranged from the serious (a bitter battle over the length of the men's downhill ski course) to the silly (an American's worry that athletes would be required to eat fish every day). The article underscores the continuing importance of one of the major goals of the Olympic games: to encourage international exchange. The nations of the world are still far from the ideal of international understanding and cooperation that the games so powerfully promote.

Throughout the history of the modern Olympic games, political differences—even the violence of terrorism and war—have added trouble to the inevitable stress of cultural differences at the games. However, the basic love of sports shared by people in all nations can triumph, as it did at the Nagano games.

Before You Read

Discuss these questions.

1. Do you enjoy watching the winter Olympics on television? Which events do you particularly enjoy?

2. Why are the Olympic games so difficult to organize and run smoothly? What sorts of difficulties and problems have you read about?

3. What do you know about Japanese customs regarding greetings and good-byes? Why might a Japanese person feel uncomfortable in social situations involving Westerners?

As You Read

As you read, try to use context clues to define the meaning of the expression "waiting for consensus" as it applies to decision making.

In Nagano, Cross-Cultural Tensions

Misunderstandings Plague Relations Between the Organizers

Reuters

1 NAGANO, Japan—Local organizers lined up in the hotel lobby with grim faces as they prepared to take a cultural leap and give a European-style kiss good-bye to representatives from the International Olympic Committee.

2 "It was embarrassing to watch," said one Japanese who witnessed the scene. "The Japanese clearly did not want to kiss anyone but felt they had to."

3 While misunderstandings over whether to kiss, shake hands or bow can be comical, other cultural gaps could have more serious consequences for the 18th Winter Olympics.

4 This may be true especially when the consensus-minded professional bureaucrats running the Olympics bump into foreign sports officials who demand instant decisions, particularly once the Games start.

5 There have already been problems, including a huge public fight over the men's downhill course, complaints about the size of hotel rooms, the number of Western-style toilets, the quality of food and criticisms about the methods for reaching decisions.

6 Makoto Kobayashi, director-general of the Nagano Organizing Committee, said cultural misunderstandings have been and will continue to be a problem.

7 Kobayashi said the bitter dispute over the start of the showpiece men's downhill was partly a result of those misunderstandings. "It was probably one of the elements," he said. "The alpine ski events which take place in Europe and the way they are prepared is probably different than the way we prepare them in Japan."

8 The dispute was finally resolved in December when Kobayashi and other organizing committee officials caved in to the pressure from international and domestic ski bodies to raise the start of the downhill.

9 International Ski Federation officials maintained that the committee's argument that raising the start would place it in a national park and thereby break environmental laws was illogical because thousands of recreational skiers already use the park every weekend during the winter.

10 "If they tell us we have violated laws, then we will accept the decision," said Gian-Franco Kasper, the ski federation's secretary-general. "But if it is because we have blond hair instead of black hair, then we will not accept it."

11 After five years of debate, a compromise was reached that put part of the course into the national park.

12 International sports executives and Nagano committee officials both said they were worried about delays in settling similar stand-offs during the Games.

13 "You have seven years to prepare and only 16 days to deliver," said Kevin Gospar, the IOC press commission chief. "We have talked about the need, when the Games are running, of flexibility. If it proves not to be working, that they will be flexible."

14 Kobayashi, a career bureaucrat in Tokyo before taking over the job of running the Olympics, said he was trying to delegate deci-

AP/Wide World Photos

The opening ceremonies for the Main Press Center in Nagano, Japan

sion-making power to lower-level officials, many of whom are government bureaucrats on loan to the Nagano committee.

15 "During the Games I have made sure all the venue managers have the authority to make decisions, because if we waited for a consensus, then the Games would not run smoothly," he said.

16 Waiting for such an agreement can be discouraging, said one foreign official working on the Nagano Organizing Committee.

17 "There are times at meetings when I just wanted to take over because it was going so slow," the official said. "A lot of visitors from overseas get frustrated because they fly over here and don't get an immediate decision."

18 The official said that while the Japanese way of waiting for a consensus often eliminated longer-term errors, there might not be enough time during the Olympics to take that approach.

19 But even Kobayashi admitted he did not embrace all Western customs, such as kissing people good-bye.

20 "I've never done it," he said. "Japanese people are very sensitive to smells and some Western women have strong perfume."

21 Kobayashi said some of the cultural gaps were based on presumptions made before people arrived here. "If they have preconceptions there is nothing we can really do about it," he said.

22 One example was a complaint by Bill Marolt, the head of the U.S. Ski and Snowboard Association, who said he was worried about Japanese food. Marolt appeared to believe the Japanese ate fish for every meal.

23 "I like fish but I'm not so sure three weeks of meals so heavy in fish and seafood would go over well with our athletes," Marolt said.

24 Kobayashi said the major hotels in the Nagano area served many different types of food, as did a 24-hour restaurant in the Olympic Village.

After reading the article, circle the best answer for each item.

1. This article was probably written
   a. before the Olympics began.
   b. in the middle of the Olympics.
   c. after the Olympics.

2. The main purpose of the article is to show that cross-cultural differences
   a. are humorous and not serious.
   b. do not exist but are misunderstandings.
   c. can cause problems in organizing an international event.

3. The local organizers were nervous about the departure of the representatives of the Olympic Committee because the Japanese
   a. do not like kissing people good-bye.
   b. did not like the Olympic Committee representatives.
   c. do not like open expressions of courtesy.

4. The most serious dispute reported in the article involved
   a. a menu for the athletes' meals.
   b. the size of the hotel rooms.
   c. the location of the ski run.

5. Before the Olympics began, some Olympic organizers were concerned that
   a. the Japanese would not welcome foreign people.
   b. the Japanese way of making decisions was too slow.
   c. Nagano businesses would not be ready for the large number of foreign visitors.

Check your answers with the key on page 117. If you have made mistakes, reread the article to gain a better understanding of it.

II. Expanding Your Vocabulary

Getting Meaning from Context

Find each word in the paragraph indicated in parentheses. Use context clues to determine the meaning of the word. Choose the definition that fits the context.

1. grim (1)   a. attractive   b. serious, unhappy

2. consensus (4, 15) a. agreement from a group   b. complete understanding

3. showpiece (7)   a. of major importance   b. overrated

4. resolved (8)	a. ended	b. done again
5. domestic (8)	a. not professional	b. not foreign
6. embrace (19)	a. criticize	b. welcome
7. sensitive (20)	a. quick to get upset	b. having a great ability to notice
8. presumptions (21)	a. beliefs	b. selfish feelings

III. Working with Idioms and Expressions

Study the meanings of these idioms and expressions. A form of each one appears in the indicated paragraph of the article.

take a leap (1) do something risky and unfamiliar

bump into (4) clash with

cave in to (8) give up, surrender

break a law (9) disobey a law

reach a compromise (11) come to an agreement by taking a middle course acceptable to both sides

take over (14, 17) gain control of

on loan to (14) temporarily lent to

Complete these sentences, using the idioms and expressions.

1. The Nagano officials did not want to raise the start of the downhill ski course, but they

   eventually decided to _____ the demands of the Ski Federation.

2. When Olympic organizers disagree, it is often best for both sides not to insist absolutely

   on one way of doing things. It is best to _____.

3. People visiting other countries will never know about the food of other cultures unless

   they sometimes _____ and try a dish they have never tried before.

4. Many local organizers work only for a limited time and are _____

   organizing committees from government offices and private corporations.

IV. Making Sense of Sentences

In each sentence or clause below, a pronoun is used to refer to a noun. Circle the noun that relates to each underlined pronoun.

1. Local organizers lined up in the hotel lobby with grim faces as <u>they</u> prepared to take a cultural leap.

2. "The alpine ski events which take place in Europe and the way they are prepared is probably different than the way we prepare <u>them</u> in Japan."

3. International Ski Federation officials maintained that the committee's argument that raising the start would place <u>it</u> in a national park and thereby break environmental laws was illogical.

4. Kobayashi, a career bureaucrat in Tokyo before taking over the job of running the Olympics, said <u>he</u> was trying to delegate decision-making power to lower-level officials.

Complete the sentences, using information from the article. For any pronouns you use, indicate the noun that the pronoun refers to.

1. Makoto Kobayashi, the head of the Nagano Organizing Committee, thought that some

   foreigners had worries about cultural issues because _____

   _____.

2. The head of the U.S. Ski and Snowboard Association complained about Japanese food

   because _____

   _____.

3. Some foreign sports officials were worried about the Japanese style of making decisions

   because _____

   _____.

4. Japanese managers at the Olympics had to be given clear authority to make decisions

   because _____

   _____.

V. Talking and Writing

Discuss the following topics. Then choose one of them to write about.

1. The article mentions the cultural preconception of an American about what the Japanese eat. What other—perhaps false—preconceptions can you think of that people have about the cuisine of various cultural groups?

2. The article begins with an awkward moment for the Japanese when they were expected to kiss foreign representatives good-bye. Have you ever encountered an awkward or confusing moment when you were with people from another culture? Describe the incident.

3. The United States refused to send athletes to the summer Olympics in Moscow in 1980 to protest the Soviet invasion of Afghanistan. And the former Soviet Union refused to send athletes to the Los Angeles summer Olympics in protest of security arrangements there. Do you think countries should use the Olympics as a means of political protest? Why or why not?

4. What is your opinion of the Olympics? Do they help to promote cultural exchanges? Are they true to their original spirit? Or are they too political or commercial?

2. Joy and Pain: The Zen of the 'Erg'

Previewing the Article

"Row, row, row your boat gently down the stream" goes the old song. But for the rowers in this article, there is no boat and no stream and those who do it "gently" are the losers.

They are enthusiasts of a new competitive indoor sport in which the athletes use rowing exercise machines while computers monitor their "distance" and speed. Rowing is a sport that is associated with picturesque rivers on beautiful spring days. The new sport seems an ironic contrast because it is done inside gymnasiums with nothing for the athletes to look at but the little computer that checks the speed. And spectators who used to stand by the banks of rivers and cheer on the athletes now stare at rows of machines that are going nowhere.

There was a time when indoor training on exercise equipment was considered preparation for the "real thing," an outdoor sport. Now, for many people, the training has become the sport itself and the basis of competition. Rowing is just one of these indoor sports. Others include "treading," or training on a treadmill; "power pumping," or weight lifting; and "spinning," or extremely fast stationary bicycling.

The word *Zen* in the headline is used in an extended sense of the word. While the strict, *denotative* meaning refers to Zen Buddhism, a religion practiced primarily in Japan, the word is sometimes used to connote an intense physical activity that brings spiritual meaning.

Before You Read

Discuss these questions.

1. Have you ever rowed, either a real boat or an exercise rowing machine? How strenuous is the activity? Do you enjoy it?

2. What is aerobic exercise? What are its benefits?

3. Do you work out? If so, do you prefer doing it in an exercise class or alone?

As You Read

A *massacre* is the killing of many people at the same time. St. Valentine's Day is February 14. The term *St. Valentine's Day Massacre* refers to a famous gang killing of seven men in Chicago on February 14, 1929. As you read, try to answer this question: Why does the author call the rowing event the St. Valentine's *Massacre* Indoor Regatta?

Joy and Pain: The Zen of the 'Erg'

By Joe Glickman
New York Times Service

1 NEW YORK—There's a standard joke among women rowers: If you can make it through an "erg" regatta, giving birth will seem easy. That's erg as in Concept II ergometer, the flywheel rowing machine that is a fixture in health clubs and is used by virtually all the roughly 1,000 rowing clubs and college crew teams in the United States. The prefix "ergo," from the Greek, means work. And as I discovered two years ago, the name fits.

2 Back then, a personal fitness trainer suggested I enter the St. Valentine's Massacre Indoor Regatta at the New York Athletic Club Boathouse on Traver's Island in Pelham, New York. I had never heard of an erg regatta, but the trainer said that my height—I'm 6 foot 4 [1.92 meters]—and background as a kayak racer would offer a distinct advantage. I decided to give it a shot.

3 My wife was somewhat less than supportive. "That's got to be the world's stupidest sporting event," she said. "Hundreds of rowers competing on gym equipment, with coaches and judges and spectators, and everyone taking it seriously?"

4 I couldn't argue that it wasn't stupid, but I was reasonably sure it wasn't the stupidest. And this Feb. 14, I'll be doing the Traver's Island regatta again. And I'm taking my 19-month-old daughter along.

5 Indoor regattas are actually quite popular. There are 38 events scheduled in the United States in 1998 and 43 on the international race calendar; the sport's own Super Bowl comes on Feb. 22 at the 16th annual World Indoor Rowing Championships in Boston.

6 This display of stationary freneticism, featuring 1,200 rowers from around the world, is known as the Crash-B Sprints, an acronym for "Charles River all-star has-beens." All races simulate 2,000 meters, the standard Olympic distance.

7 Erg enthusiasts who choose not to enter a regatta can join the fray by submitting their best time to Concept II, the machine's manufacturer, for the world rankings. The 1997 list included 18,000 rowers from 56 countries. Of course, as my grandmother used to say, and my wife would concur, just because something's popular doesn't mean it's not stupid. But those of us hooked on this sport are willing to suffer the jibes of skeptics and spouses.

Paula Lerner/The Picture Cube

At the World Indoor Rowing Championship of 1993.

8 The Concept II machine was invented in 1981 by Peter and Dick Dreissigacker, oar makers and brothers from Orange, Connecticut, who started by nailing Dick's inverted bicycle to the floor. The current edition is nearly 8 feet long with a contoured seat that slides on the aluminum rail as an oarsman would in a rowing shell. The performance monitor—the mute coxswain who never lies—gives digital feedback on average pace, total distance and time.

9 The intensity of the workout is in your control. The harder you pull, the more resistance you feel, just as you would on the water.

10 The erg works the whole body—legs, arms, back, abs and buttocks—more muscle mass than any other piece of indoor gym equipment, providing a very efficient total-body workout. Rowing is one of the few aerobic activities that can strengthen your lower back. And since rowing is impact-free, it can be done well past one's competitive prime.

11 I had six weeks to train for my first erg regatta. The workouts devised by my trainer-friend were surprisingly short: 30 minutes at 70 percent of my maximum heart rate, 15 minutes at 80 percent, and four intervals of 2 minutes all-out, with 2 minutes' rest in between. Within a few weeks, my legs and lungs started to respond.

12 On Valentine's Day, I kissed my wife good-bye and headed off to the massacre. As I approached the New York Athletic Club Boathouse, overlooking Long Island Sound, the din of the crowd seeped through the walls. The chilly gym, sporting the flags of college crew teams, was packed with hundreds of tall, muscular jocks in crew-team jackets cheering on their teammates.

13 A rope sectioned off 16 brand-new ergs sitting side by side. Heats went off in measured intervals: heavyweights, lightweights, men and women, juniors, open, masters. Each ergometer was hooked up to a computer monitored by an official.

14 Rowers struggle to compare the whole-body pain of oxygen debt with anything else they've experienced in sports. One West Point cadet with crossed oars tattooed on his sinewy back said: "We describe the pain as excruciating, or excruciating plus. When you're finished, you're shot, because you've given it your all. And then you think, I could have kicked it in the last 600 meters instead of 500. There's always another level of pain you can get to. It's a bit sick."

15 Sick or pure? Masochistic or self-transcendent? At the competitive level, pain is part of most sports: running, swimming, cycling. In an activity with minimal technique and no locomotion, erg racing is pain unadorned.

16 My division was heavyweight masters, with about 40 competitors aged 30 to 39. After an anxious wait, the gun went off, and I pulled. With the crowd and adrenaline, the first two minutes felt easy, despite the fact that I was going faster than I ever had. Two minutes later, my lower back hurt, my hamstrings burned, my lungs really, really hurt, and I was slowing down.

17 With 800 meters to go, lactic acid surged through my self-deluded veins. I heard the crowd urging me on. "You're ahead," came the cry. "Pull!"

18 After what seemed like an eternity, I was done. My time for 2,000 meters was 6 minutes 20.3 seconds. I slumped over, a wheezing shell. But when I looked up, I noticed that everyone else was still rowing. I had won!

19 What a great sport.

I. Getting the Message

After reading the article, circle the best answer for each item.

1. "Erg" is
   a. a traditional name for a kind of boat race.
   b. a short name for an exercise machine.
   c. the name for a strenuous exercise workout.

2. One sign that the writer has been involved in athletics is that he
   a. was once a kayak racer.
   b. trained for the regatta.
   c. includes many facts about indoor racing.

3. The writer's wife thinks that indoor rowing competitions are
   a. exciting.
   b. a nice tradition.
   c. stupid.

4. According to the author, rowing on the Concept II machine feels
   a. very different from rowing a real boat.
   b. like riding a bicycle.
   c. similar to rowing a boat.

5. The writer's precontest workout training schedule was
   a. probably a very good one.
   b. probably a very bad one.
   c. created by the writer himself.

6. At the end of the competition, the writer was
   a. angry and depressed.
   b. relaxed but upset.
   c. in pain but happy.

7. The erg regatta is like regular boating competitions because
   a. winning means going the fastest over a set "distance."
   b. winning means beating one's own best time.
   c. it is a team sport, not an individual sport.

Check your answers with the key on page 117. If you have made mistakes, reread the article to gain a better understanding of it.

II. Expanding Your Vocabulary

A. Getting Meaning from Context

Find each word in the paragraph indicated in parentheses. Use context clues to determine the meaning of the word. Choose the definition that fits the context.

1. fixture (1)   a. something not broken   b. something commonly found

2. stationary (6)   a. not moving   b. loud

3. freneticism (6)   a. great fear   b. great excitement

4. simulate (6)   a. encourage   b. copy

5. concur (7)   a. agree   b. argue

6. jibes (7)   a. silly statements   b. unkind statements

7. inverted (8)   a. big   b. upside-down

8. din (12)   a. an impressive sight   b. a loud noise

9. excruciating (14)   a. very strong   b. not noticeable

10. masochistic (15)   a. causing pain to oneself   b. causing pain to others

B. Identifying Categories of Words

Find the term that doesn't belong in each category. Look up any words you don't know in a dictionary.

1. categories of competitors

   heavyweights   **lightweights**   **skeptics**   **juniors**

2. nonparticipants at an indoor boating race

   judges   **spectators**   **coaches**   **meters**

3. parts of the body that benefit from rowing

   back   **arms**   **abs (abdominal muscles)**   **aerobics**

4. names for indoor regatta competitors

   erg enthusiasts   **rowers**   **oarsmen**   **gymnasts**

5. a thing that a person can row

   ergometer   **kayak**   **shell**   **feedback**

III. Working with Idioms and Expressions

Study the meanings of these idioms and expressions. A form of each one appears in the indicated paragraph of the article.

make it through (1) succeed; last

give something a shot (2) try something

take something seriously (3) do something sincerely and earnestly

join the fray (7) become involved in the fight or contest

be hooked on (7) be dedicated to; have a strong habit that one is unable to break

head off (12) leave to go someplace

be hooked up (13) be connected to

be shot (14) be totally exhausted

give something your all (14) try as hard as you can

Answer these questions.

1. Why do some people get *hooked on* the Concept II machine?

2. Did the writer of the article *give* the indoor rowing competition *his all*?

3. Did the writer's wife *join the fray* at the indoor regatta competition?

4. *Was* the writer *shot* at the end of the competition?

IV. Focusing on Style and Tone

The author's purpose in this article is to inform the reader about an unusual sporting event. Instead of using the objective style of a feature writer, he uses the personal style of the essayist—and he does this with a humorous tone. These characteristics—informative purpose, personal style, and humorous tone—can be seen in the introductory and concluding paragraphs of the article.

Answer the following questions.

1. Why does the author begin the article with a joke? Is this a good way to begin?

2. What does the writer mean by this statement in paragraph 1: "And as I discovered two years ago, the name fits"? Does this make the reader curious about what is coming in the rest of the article? Why?

3. What statistic does the writer use in the first paragraph to inform the reader about how popular the rowing machine is?

4. What information does the author put in the final four paragraphs of the article? Why do you think he leaves this information for the end? How does this information lead to a *climax* for the article?

5. Why does the writer say, in the last line of the article, "What a great sport"? Why is this funny in view of his wife's evaluation of the sport?

V. Talking and Writing

Discuss the following topics. Then choose one of them to write about.

1. Write two reasons that indoor rowing could be called a "stupid" sport. Then write two reasons that it could be called a "good" sport. Which point of view is your own? Why?

2. Do you prefer playing individual sports or team sports? Do you prefer playing a sport indoors or outdoors? Explain your answers.

3. What sport do you enjoy the most as a spectator? Why? Do you think you would enjoy watching indoor rowing?

3. At Last, Women Toss the Sequins

Previewing the Article

Think of women on ice at the Olympics, and most people think of graceful young women figure skaters in elegant costumes with flashing sequins. These women perform athletic jumps and balletic twirls on ice, and typically their events are among the hottest tickets at the Olympics.

But now people are going to have to revise this image of women on ice. At the 1998 Olympics at Nagano, Japan (see the article on their organization, "In Nagano, Cross-Cultural Tensions," in this section), women's hockey was played as a team sport for the first time in Olympic history. In contrast to the graceful elegance of figure skating, when people think of hockey, they think of hefty men knocking one another down to the ice–and even engaging in fistfights. So there was a great deal of curiosity about the event—and a good deal of adjusting of the image of women on ice.

As this article shows, the sport was in the spotlight because it was a first. And the United States team, mentioned prominently in this article, did go home with the first Olympic gold medal in the sport.

The following information will help you read the article with greater understanding:

- *Body checking* is a hockey term that refers to blocking or stopping an opposing player by using one's body.

- *Roughing penalty* is a punishment given to a hockey player for being deliberately violent. Usually the player is out of the game for a period of time, during which the team plays with one fewer player.

- An *assist* is a pass to another player who then scores a goal by hitting the puck into the net past the *goalie*. When the goalie stops the puck from entering the goal, it's a *save*.

- A *triple toe-loop* is a jump in figure skating in which the skater makes three turns in the air.

Before You Read

1. What do you know about ice hockey? What is your image of the sport? How is ice hockey like other kinds of hockey?

2. Women's team sports have not typically had the high profile of men's team sports. How is that changing? Why is hockey considered a nontraditional sport for women?

As You Read

Look for information on how women's hockey is different from men's hockey.

At Last, Women Can Toss the Sequins

By Kevin Sullivan
Washington Post Service

Olivier Morin/Agence France-Presse

Elizabeth Brown, a U.S. forward, fighting off opponents during the U.S. victory over China on Sunday.

1   NAGANO—Female skaters are the marquee athletes at the Olympics, the household names with faces and stories that dominate prime-time coverage of the Olympics. But those women have always been the ones wearing figure skates and sequins and stage make-up. On Sunday night, female athletes wearing shoulder pads and face masks and steel-toed hockey skates proved that there is more to graceful skating than triple toe-loops.

2   A new breed of women on ice introduced itself to the Olympics on Sunday as the United States scrapped and slapped its way to a lopsided, 5-0 victory over China on the first day of women's hockey in Olympic history.

3   The American women's team, one of the top U.S. medal contenders, dominated the Chinese on a day that opened opportunities beyond figure skating for young girls everywhere who dream of Olympic gold.

4   "It's not just a man's game anymore," said Cammi Granato, the U.S. team captain, who scored twice. "We really feel like we're out here paving the way for all the women behind us."

5   Women's hockey is making its Olympic debut after decades of relative obscurity. While it has been largely overshadowed at these Games by Olympic men's hockey, which will have all the stars from the National Hockey League for the first time, the women's game is one of the most popular and watched additions to Olympic competition.

6   "I think this is doing a lot for young girls; they have a lot more dreams now," said Jenny Schmidgall, 18, a U.S. forward who had a goal and an assist Sunday and will enter the University of Minnesota this autumn to play on the school's first women's hockey team.

7   In every Olympic games, a new sport emerges as the "hip" game of the moment.

In Nagano, snowboarding and women's hockey have captured imaginations of athletes and spectators. Granato and her teammates, mostly well-spoken products of New England colleges, have been swamped by news organizations from around the world. Sue Merz, of Greenwich, Connecticut, a defender who played hockey in Switzerland after graduating from college, was interviewed by a Swiss television station in German.

8   "Our top priority is to win a medal," Merz said. "But for all those young girls out there, they can look at these women playing and say, 'I want to be like that, Mom.'"

9   Women's hockey is markedly different from the men's game. Skating is slower and shooting is weaker, but it is played with great skill by the top teams here. The Americans played a precision passing game that gave them almost continuous possession of the puck. The Americans outshot the Chinese, 31-10, and the U.S. goalie, Sarah Tueting, did not make a save that required pads until the third period.

10   Body-checking is illegal, so there is none of the violent crashing and banging that television viewers are accustomed to when watching men play. An American player was given a roughing penalty for a slap that was probably softer than the one she got from the doctor when she was born.

11   The women are also smaller than the men, but a lot bigger than their figure skating counterparts. The heaviest player on the U.S. team is Angela Ruggiero, a 175-pound defender who weighs five pounds more than Jason Dungjen, the heaviest

U.S. male figure skater. The lightest player, 127-pound forward Alana Blahoski, is still a lot bigger than the 79-pound figure skating sensation Tara Lipinski.

12   The Americans' crushing victory over China shows that women's hockey is still wildly uneven, with Canada and the United States, the No. 1 and 2 seeds in Nagano, dominating world play and other countries lagging far behind in a tournament that numbers only six teams. Canada crushed Japan on Sunday by the football-like score of 13-0, and Finland defeated Sweden by a touchdown, 6-0. That means the three top teams won by a combined score of 24 to nothing.

13   Although the U.S.-China game was even more one-sided than the score suggests, fans in the cavernous Aqua Wave rink, which looks like a hangar for jumbo jets, were still excited. A large contingent from the United States waved flags and screamed for the U.S. women.

14   "I think about girls growing up and knowing that there are more options for them than just figure skating," said Christina Dunn, 28, from Massachusetts, whose sister, Tricia, plays on the U.S. team. "These women are showing them that they can do something maybe a little more non-traditional."

15   Heather Norton, 23, from Maine, who played hockey at the University of New Hampshire, called the game "historic."

16   "So many women have spent their lives breaking down the barriers between men's and women's sports and breaking down old stereotypes," Norton said. "This game should have happened a long time ago."

A. Reading for Key Ideas

After reading the article, circle the best answer for each item.

1. The women's hockey teams were a center of attention at the 1998 Olympics because
   a. professional players played on them for the first time.
   b. teams competed for the first time for medals.
   c. teams competed with men's teams for the first time.

2. Men's hockey teams were different at the 1998 Olympics because they
   a. included stars from professional teams.
   b. became a center of attention for the first time.
   c. played the game more violently than ever before.

3. Sue Merz, a player on the United States women's hockey team, thinks that
   a. the United States team will win a medal.
   b. women's hockey at the Olympics will help lead more girls to enter nontraditional sports.
   c. women's hockey games are too violent.

4. In the 1998 Olympics, in the women's hockey competition,
   a. teams were fairly equal, and the scores were close.
   b. teams from Europe were the strongest.
   c. a few teams were much stronger than the others.

5. According to Christina Dunn, ice hockey is
   a. a more appropriate sport for women than figure skating.
   b. a sport that women didn't use to play much but may in the future.
   c. not a good choice of sport for young women because of its violence.

Check your answers with the key on page 117. If you have made mistakes, reread the article to gain a better understanding of it.

B. Reading for Details

In the article much information is given about the differences between men's and women's hockey. Indicate whether each statement is true (**T**) or false (**F**).

1. _____ Women's hockey is different from men's hockey in that it doesn't have a goalie.

2. _____ Women's hockey is faster than men's hockey.

3. _____ Women's hockey is less violent than men's hockey.

4. _____ The physical move of body checking is not legal in women's hockey.

5. _____ Women hockey players have less skill in passing than male players.

6. _____ Women hockey players' shots on the goal are weaker than men's.

7. _____ Women's hockey was as popular and well-watched as men's hockey at the 1998 Olympics.

II. Expanding Your Vocabulary

A. Getting Meaning from Context

Find each word in the paragraph indicated in parentheses. Use context clues to determine the meaning of the word. Choose the definition that fits the context.

1. breed (2)   a. type   b. herd

2. contenders (3)   a. supporters   b. participants in a contest

3. overshadowed (5)   a. made less visible   b. become dark

4. swamped (7)   a. overwhelmed   b. ignored

5. counterparts (11)   a. people with the same job b. opponents in a contest

6. sensation (11)   a. an outstanding person   b. a strong feeling

7. one-sided (13)   a. dominated by one team   b. unfair and biased

8. contingent (13)   a. a group   b. contestants

B. Finding Verbs with Similar Meanings

Find a verb with a similar meaning in the paragraph indicated in parentheses.

1. *are the most prominent* (1) _____

2. *showed* (1) _____

3. *appears* (7) _____

4. *beat by a large score* (12) _____

5. *indicates* (13) _____

III. Working with Idioms and Expressions

Answer these questions with **yes** or **no**. Pay particular attention to the meanings of the expressions in **bold** print. Each expression appears in the indicated paragraph of the article. Explain your answers.

1. If a performer is a **marquee figure** (1), does the person get large audiences? _____

2. The women hockey players feel they are **paving the way** (4) for women in sports. Are they afraid that they are making it harder for women in the future? _____

3. If a person **makes a debut** (5) onstage, has the person appeared onstage before?

   _____

4. If some teams in the hockey tournament **lag far behind**, (12) is the difference in strength between the top teams and the bottom teams very great? _____

IV. Making Sense of Sentences

To describe women's and men's hockey, the author uses many expressions of comparison. These include comparative and superlative forms. Comparative forms take –er endings or the word *more*. Superlatives take –est endings or the word *most*.

Women's figure skating is *more popular* than women's speed skating. (comparative adjective form)

The winter Olympics have *more* sports than ever before. (comparative with a noun)

Women's hockey is one of the *newest* sports in the Olympics. (superlative form)

Answer these questions with comparative or superlative forms. Look for the answers in the paragraphs indicated in parentheses.

1. What kind of addition to the Olympic games is women's hockey? (5) _____

   _____

2. How does women's skating in ice hockey compare with men's skating in the sport? (9)

   _____

3. How does women's shooting compare with men's shooting? (9) _____

_____

4. What does Christina Dunn say about the options for ice sports that there are for girls

growing up? (14) _____

Reread paragraph 11. Then number the athletes in order from smallest to largest.

_____ the heaviest female U.S. hockey team member

_____ the lightest U.S. female hockey player

_____ male hockey players

_____ the heaviest U.S. male figure skater

___1___ a top female figure skater

V. Talking and Writing

Discuss the following topics. Then choose one of them to write about.

1. Do you watch sports on TV? Which sports do you prefer to watch? Do you like to watch women's sports? Which do you like to watch?

2. How are traditional barriers breaking down between men and women in sports? What examples do you know of?

3. How are traditional barriers breaking down between men and women in the United States and other countries in the home and in business? What experiences have taken place in your parents' lifetime? your lifetime?

4. In the past, colleges in the United States put overwhelming emphasis on, and money into, men's sports. Now the situation is changing and women's sports are receiving more money. What do you know about this situation? What is your opinion of it?

Focus on the Newspaper

Who won the freestyle women's skating competition in the winter Olympics? What teams will be the strongest in the next World Cup soccer tournament? Currently, who is the world's fastest human? Most newspapers have a daily sports section that answers questions such as these.

Contents of Sports Articles

Much of the information on the sports pages is transitory: it is of interest for the current day and may be of little interest the following day. Sports articles tell the results of yesterday's games and the prospects for today's and tomorrow's games.

Sports feature articles, however, tackle larger issues, such as the roles of business and politics in sports. Other feature articles give insight into the sport itself or into the people who play the sport. Some articles, however, like the three articles in this section, are of more lasting interest. The article about the Nagano winter Olympics, for example, reveals the interesting way people from different parts of the world dealt with cultural clashes in preparation for the games. In addition, the article about indoor rowing will remain an entertaining personal look at a sport for a long time to come.

Exercise 1: Who's the Winner?

Choose two or three articles from the sports section of a newspaper and analyze their contents. Decide what type of article each one is, and answer the appropriate questions in the box titled "Analyzing a Sports Article."

Analyzing a Sports Article

1. What is the sport?

2. What's the headline? What key words help you predict the content of the article?

3. Does a photo accompany the article? If so, what does it show?

4. What is the purpose of the article? Does it report the results of a contest or analyze one about to take place? Or is it a feature article?

Articles on Sports Results

1. What was the contest?

2. Where and when did the contest take place?

3. Was there a key play or player?

---

4. Is the contest discussed in strict chronological order?

Articles on Future Sports Events

1. What is the contest?

2. Where and when will the contest take place?

3. What are the predictions for the outcome?

4. What is the importance of the contest?

Sports Feature Articles

1. What is the topic of the article?

2. Does the article address issues other than sports (for example, finances or health)? If so, which ones?

Profiles of Sports Figures

1. Why did the newspaper print a feature about this person at this time?

2. Does the article portray this person sympathetically or unsympathetically? What sentences give you the best clues?

3. Does the article make you want to read more about this person? Why or why not?

The Language of Sports

Exercise 2: Sports Vocabulary

Each sport has its own terminology. Pick a sport that you know. Look at several newspaper articles about the sport. Make a list of terms relating to the sport. Arrange them in categories such as the ones listed below. Add or delete categories as appropriate.

positions on the field	_____
plays	_____
verbs (action words)	_____
slang	_____
other	_____

Share your list with your classmates. Compare your list with those of other students who chose the same sport.

COMPREHENSION CHECK

Answers to "Getting the Message" Exercises

Section 1:
News/Features

Article 1 (page 4)
1. b
2. a
3. c
4. a
5. b
6. c
7. a

Article 2 (page 10)
1. F
2. F
3. F
4. T
5. F
6. T
7. F
8. F

Section 2:
Opinion

Article 1 (page 20)
1. b
2. c
3. a
4. c
5. b

Article 2 (page 25)
1. T
2. T
3. T
4. F
5. T
6. T
7. T
8. F

Section 3:
Business

Article 1 (page 34)
A.
1. c
2. a
3. a
4. a
5. b
6. b
B.
1. cave
2. cube
3. cube
4. cave
5. cave
6. cube

Article 2 (page 40)
1. a
2. b
3. b
4. c
5. b

Section 4:
Profiles

Article 1 (page 48)
A.
1. F
2. T
3. T
4. F
5. T
6. F
7. F
8. T
B.
1. yes
2. not given
3. no
4. yes
5. no
6. not given
7. no

8. no
9. not given
10. not given

Article 2 (page 54)
1. b
2. b
3. c
4. b
5. a

Section 5:
Arts/Entertainment

Article 1 (page 64)
1. F
2. T
3. T
4. T
5. T
6. F
7. F

Article 2 (page 69)
1. c
2. b
3. c
4. c
5. a

Article 3 (page 75)
1. b
2. a
3. a
4. c
5. c

Section 6:
Science/Health

Article 1 (page 84)
1. c
2. a
3. b
4. a
5. b
6. a

Article 2 (page 90)
1. T
2. F
3. T
4. T
5. F
6. F
7. T

Section 7:
Sports

Article 1 (page 98)
1. a
2. c
3. a
4. c
5. b

Article 2 (page 104)
1. b
2. a
3. c
4. c
5. a
6. c
7. a

Article 3 (page 110)
A.
1. b
2. a
3. b
4. c
5. b
B.
1. F
2. F
3. T
4. T
5. F
6. T
7. F